THE HEALTHY MEAL PREP INSTANT POT® COOKBOOK

the Healthy Meal Prep
Instant Pot® COOKBOOK

No-Fuss Recipes for Nutritious, Ready-to-Go Meals

CARRIE FORREST MBA, MPH

Photography by Marija Vidal

ROCKRIDGE PRESS

Interior and Cover Designer: Emma Hall
Art Producer: Sue Smith
Editor: Clara Song Lee
Production Editor: Erum Khan
Photography © 2019 Marija Vidal. Food styling by Cregg Green.
Author photo courtesy of Amy Wellenkamp.
Cover: Balsamic Chicken with Vegetables and Potatoes

ISBN: Print 978-1-64152-425-4 | eBook 978-1-64152-426-1

TO ALAN,
for showing me that what you dream, you can achieve.

CONTENTS

INTRODUCTION

AS A BUSY FOOD BLOGGER AND CLEAN-EATING SPECIALIST, come six o'clock in the evening, I'm ready to plop down on the sofa and have a healthy meal magically appear in front of me. Yet, magical elves have never appeared ready to serve my dinner. That's where the Instant Pot® and meal prepping comes in.

When I got my first Instant Pot® more than two years ago, I finally had the answer to my dinner prep dilemma. Additionally, since the Instant Pot® is ideal for making a larger number of portions, my total time spent in the kitchen is reduced by strategically cooking in bulk and then repurposing the leftovers over the next few days. Turns out, the Instant Pot® is the magical answer I was looking for!

Cooking at home has helped me stay healthy, too. Before I learned how to cook and knew much about nutrition, I ate mostly packaged foods full of preservatives and processed ingredients. My health really suffered. By the time I reached my early 30s, I had developed a long list of serious health problems that negatively impacted my life. I had uncontrollable anxiety and panic attacks, migraines, digestive problems, and hormone imbalance. It got to the point where I had a hard time being social, and I wasn't even sure if I could work anymore.

Transforming my health started with cleaning up my diet. I bought fresh ingredients instead of processed. At first it felt overwhelming, but I took it one step at a time. I tried my best to make cleaner food choices by eating more fruits, vegetables, beans, eggs, meats, fish, poultry, nuts, and seeds. Before long, I started feeling better. The health symptoms that had been so debilitating diminished and, in some cases, completely went away.

Over the years, I picked up various tips and tricks to make meals that are as delicious as they are healthy. For example, fresh herbs and dried spices are great ways to amplify both the flavors and nutrient content of basic foods. It's also important to add healthy fats—like avocado and coconut—to keep you fuller for longer and to help your body absorb essential fat-soluble vitamins. I'm a firm believer that healthy food can and should taste good.

In *The Healthy Meal Prep Instant Pot® Cookbook*, you'll find:

- A carefully curated collection of healthy, nutritious recipes that are delicious, easy to prepare, and suited to advance meal prep

- Tips for advance prepping that indicate when you can premeasure and store ingredients so they can be cooked later at a moment's notice

- Practical tips to incorporate healthy recipes into a weekly meal prep plan

- Substitutions to make recipes suitable for dairy-free, gluten-free, vegetarian, and vegan diets

Whether you're at the beginning of your health journey or you're just looking for satisfying, clean-eating recipes, I'm so glad you're here. I'm excited to share how easy and enjoyable it can be to make great food at home. Let's get started!

Healthy Food in an Instant

To prepare healthy foods, it's important to understand the basics of how to cook them in the Instant Pot®. Since the Instant Pot® is ideal for meal prepping, knowing which foods can be prepped and cooked several days in advance makes breakfast, lunch, and dinner a snap on days that are particularly busy.

Smart Technology for Healthy Meals

I bought my Instant Pot® in 2016 after seeing more and more Instant Pot® recipes pop up online. It wasn't long before I posted a few simple ones on my blog. They were a huge hit, and more and more people came to my blog just to get those recipes. It seemed like everyone appreciated easy, healthy meals that could be made super fast.

CLEAN, NUTRITIOUS FOOD

The recipes in this book follow clean-eating guidelines—in other words, they call for unprocessed ingredients as often as possible. This means using foods that are in their natural form, such as fruits, vegetables, beans, whole grains, meat, fish, poultry, eggs, nuts, and seeds. "Clean eating" is a term that is meant to be flexible to allow for individual dietary preferences and needs, including vegetarian and vegan, dairy-free, and gluten-free. Recipes include tips for these diets wherever possible.

When it comes to planning meals, nutrition experts agree that a balanced approach works best. From snacks to full dinners—all should include a combination of protein, fat, and carbohydrates. A good rule of thumb is to fill at least half of your plate with raw or cooked nonstarchy vegetables, one-fourth with lean protein, and the last fourth with complex carbohydrates such as cooked squash or potato, whole grains, or fruit. A few tablespoons of a healthy fat such as avocado helps you feel satisfied and helps your body absorb the nutrients from the other foods in your meal.

Meal prep makes putting a healthy dinner on the table a much easier task, reducing your likelihood to grab for those processed foods and opt for takeout. Further, I'm less likely to overeat home-cooked meals as opposed to foods prepared outside my kitchen. By planning and preparing your own foods, you have control over portion size and the quality of your ingredients, both of which are very important aspects of clean, healthy eating.

The Instant Pot® is ideal for healthy cooking because the pressure and steam created by the boiling liquid cook food faster than on the stovetop or in the oven, without sacrificing nutrients or food quality. Pressure cooking is also healthier than other cooking processes that use high heat, such as grilling, baking, and frying, which can create harmful carcinogens.

RISE OF THE INSTANT POT®

The practice of cooking foods under pressure has actually been around for hundreds of years. Pressure cooking didn't become mainstream in the United States until the 1950s, though, when more women went to work and needed efficient ways to prepare family meals.

Fast forward to the Instant Pot® debut in 2009. Engineers created an appliance that was super easy and safe to use, with pre-programmed buttons and built-in safety features. It wasn't long before the Instant Pot® (affectionately known as "the IP") became a hit with home cooks, and it remains all the rage today. Need proof? Look no further than its sales topping the Amazon Prime Day charts for the last several years.

This book focuses on meal-prep-friendly recipes entirely made in the Instant Pot®. It's all about quickly prepping ingredients, tossing them into the IP, pushing a few buttons, and letting it do its magic. You'll feel good about serving home-cooked meals that use healthy ingredients and cause you a lot less stress.

SUPER EASY RECIPES

The Instant Pot® is ideal for making healthy meals in bulk and then refrigerating or freezing them for later. Each recipe was created with this strategy in mind. To make things even easier, many recipes are one pot, freezer friendly, and advance prep friendly.

It's equally important that ingredients are easy to find and affordable. As you work through the recipes in this book, you won't have to search for obscure items or unfamiliar spices. In fact, many of the recipes include the option to use frozen produce, which makes it easy to prepare certain foods even when they're not in season. Other budget-friendly and healthy ingredients used throughout include grains, beans, and whole-grain pasta.

Using an Instant Pot®

The Instant Pot® is essentially made up of six pieces:

1. The main base where the panel and buttons are located

2. The stainless-steel inner pot

3. The lid with the steam release knob

4. The sealing ring inside the lid

5. A stainless steel trivet (used in some but not all recipes)

6. The electric cord that plugs in the back of the base

The main base with the panel and all the buttons can be intimidating, but you actually need to use only a few settings to get started:

PRESSURE LEVEL. Make sure it is set to High.

PRESSURE COOK OR MANUAL. Use the up and down buttons to set the time your recipe indicates.

CANCEL. Hit this button if you need to stop the cooking process.

Here are the general steps for making most recipes in the Instant Pot®:

1. Add your ingredients, including at least 1 cup of liquid.

2. Lock the lid into place. Make sure the steam release knob is in the sealed position.

3. Set the cooking time and the pressure to High (most common) or Low.

4. After cooking, release the pressure.

5. Unlock and remove the lid. Serve your food.

Here are a few other tips to keep in mind as you get started:

- You'll always need at least 1 cup of liquid to cook anything in your Instant Pot®.
- After sautéing, use a wooden spoon to scrape up any bits of food stuck to the bottom of the pot. This will prevent you from getting a Burn message.
- Most recipes call for a natural release, quick release, or a combination of the two.
  - → Quick release means a lot of steam, so use tongs or an oven mitt to avoid burning your fingers.
  - → Natural pressure release means letting the pressure come down by itself after cooking is complete. This usually takes about 15 minutes.
  - → Some recipes call for a natural release for 10 minutes, then quick releasing any remaining pressure. You won't be able to unlock the lid until all the steam has been released.

Cook Once, Eat Many Times

Meal prepping is a game changer for busy people who want to eat healthy. Even if you love to cook, sometimes there just isn't enough time in the day to make a healthy meal from scratch. When I have at least a few recipes prepped and waiting for me in the fridge, I'm less likely to grab something on the go or order out. This saves me money and helps me stay on track with my healthy eating goals.

MEAL PREP BASICS

With meal prepping, you can choose how much you want to make in advance, from one meal to a whole week's worth. You can also batch cook, preparing some ingredients ahead of time, such as proteins, potatoes, beans, and grains. Batch cooking is helpful because it makes day-to-day cooking easier. This style of meal prepping is also known as "buffet-style" meal prep and allows for a flexible, mix-and-match approach to breakfasts, lunches, and dinners throughout the week ahead. (See chapter 2 for a bunch of make-ahead staples and basics.)

Additionally, you can always advance prep your ingredients for recipes you are going to make later. Ingredients can be premeasured and pre-chopped and stored in jars or zip-top bags so it's much easier to make a specific recipe later in the week. Advance prepping is a great way to get children involved with meal planning, too, since even young kids can help with tasks like washing vegetables.

REPURPOSING LEFTOVERS

All of the recipes in this book reheat very well. If you prefer to cook every night, then leftovers can be refrigerated for lunch the next day or frozen to have at a later date. Leftovers are wonderfully versatile, especially when you bulk-cook staples like beans, rice, and potatoes. For example:

- Form leftover cooked lentils into patties for a burger alternative, or sauté them with sliced onion and red bell peppers to make lentil taco "meat."

- Shred extra cooked chicken for chicken tacos or chicken salad.

- Combine some cooked brown rice with steamed vegetables for a simple casserole or with cooked lentils to make vegetarian "meatloaf."

- Serve steamed vegetables with butter or your favorite vinaigrette. Vegetables can be reheated in a skillet with cooked chicken and vegetables or sautéed with sliced beef and teriyaki sauce for a quick stir-fry.

HEALTHY MEAL PREP RECIPES

The recipes in this book are not only great for healthy lifestyles they're meal-prep-friendly as well.

- Many recipes are easy to cook in bulk, and store and reheat very well.

- There are recipes noted as **freezer friendly**, meaning they freeze well and can be served later.

- Recipes labeled **one pot** indicate when an entire meal can be made in the Instant Pot®, no other equipment needed. That also makes them super easy to clean up, so they're ideal for busy days.

- **Advance prep** tips explain how to get the ingredients ready ahead of time; **meal prep** tips share ways to reheat or repurpose the dish and other recipes that pair well with it.

Step-by-Step Meal Prep

Here's a basic guide to get started. Once you master the strategy, check out the Sample Five-Recipe Meal Prep Plan on page 10 for a more in-depth example of meal prepping in action.

STEP 1: Plan which recipes you want to make. I recommend keeping a calendar with meal ideas for the week. A small whiteboard in the kitchen works great, as does your phone.

STEP 2: Make sure you have enough storage containers for the food you make. I prefer glass containers with airtight lids. If you plan to use plastic containers, they should be food safe and BPA free.

STEP 3: Shop for ingredients. You can usually get better pricing on dry ingredients like beans and rice when you buy them in bulk. Stock up on frozen and canned items, too (I choose reduced-sodium options whenever possible).

STEP 4: Cook a few recipes in bulk, starting with the one that takes the longest to cook. While the first one is cooking, prep ingredients for the remaining recipes so you can start the next one as soon as the first one is finished.

STEP 5: Store the meals. I write the date I cooked each recipe on a piece of masking tape on each container so I don't keep it longer than intended. Most cooked foods stored in the fridge should be eaten within 4 days. Frozen foods can usually last up to several months.

STEP 6: Most prepared foods can be reheated in the microwave or on the stovetop. For best results, thaw frozen food overnight in the refrigerator. Before reheating, I add about a teaspoon of water to the microwave-safe container with my food and cover it with plastic wrap. I poke a few holes in the plastic and heat the food for 45 to 90 seconds or until it is steaming. To reheat on the stovetop, transfer the food to a medium saucepan with about a teaspoon of water. Reheat over medium heat until the food is simmering.

Pot-in-Pot (PIP) Cooking

Pot-in-pot cooking means cooking in another vessel inside the inner pot. I recommend an ovenproof 7- or 8-inch ceramic soufflé dish or glass bowl (1½ to 2 quart capacity) that fits into either a 6- or 8-quart Instant Pot®. PIP cooking is ideal for making quiches or casseroles or cooking two separate items at once.

For PIP cooking, you'll need a sling to lower and lift the dish onto and off of the trivet. To make a sling, fold two 2-foot-long pieces of aluminum foil in half, and then fold them in half again. This creates two slender, long strips of foil. Arrange the strips in a plus sign shape. Place the baking dish in the center of the plus sign, and bend the foil strips upward to make two sets of handles. Use these handles to place the dish on the trivet inside the inner pot and to lift it out after cooking.

The Instant Pot® Meal Prep Guide

I love to eat, but I don't love spending hours in the kitchen. The good news is that the Instant Pot® has some amazing features to make your meal prep time as fast and efficient as possible.

HOW TO MULTITASK WITH A MULTICOOKER

The Instant Pot® was designed to make your life easier, but there are additional ways to make it even more efficient. Here are some of my favorite multitasking tips:

- The Instant Pot® is more than a pressure cooker. It has a Slow Cook option that allows you to make foods that benefit from low and slow cooking, such as a lean roast or homemade bone broth. Slow cook overnight or while you're at work for optimal efficiency.

- Most Instant Pot® models have a Keep Warm mode, which keeps the cooked food at a safe temperature for several hours until you're ready to eat it or pack it up for later.

- If you're cooking foods that have similar cook times, use the trivet to cook multiple foods at once. For example, chicken breasts and potatoes take about the same amount of time. Place the trivet in the inner pot, add a cup of water, and cook a couple of chicken breasts and potatoes at the same time.

- Purchase an extra stainless steel inner pot. This allows you to move quickly from one recipe to the next, especially when you're meal prepping.

SAMPLE FIVE-RECIPE MEAL PREP PLAN

Here's a sample strategy for prepping five meals on the weekend to last through the first half of the week ahead. I generally pick two main dishes, one side dish, one staple, and one breakfast. You can then pick another three or four recipes to cook in the middle of the week, which will take you through to the weekend. I recommend cooking these recipes in the order they are listed. While the first recipe is cooking, prep ingredients for the other recipes so you'll be ready to start the next one right away.

- Broccoli and Cheddar Crustless Quiche (page 43). This is perfect for breakfast, and the leftovers can be served for lunch.

- Teriyaki Chicken and Rice (page 130). This is a great basic to have on hand, and both kids and adults love it. Serve it for lunch or dinner along with steamed broccoli and carrots.

- Sloppy Joes (page 152). These are traditionally served on hamburger buns, but they're also delicious over sweet potatoes, mashed potatoes, or rice.

- Sweet Potatoes (page 27). I always have a batch of cooked sweet potatoes in my fridge because they are both cheap and highly nutritious. They can be served plain or with butter and are a healthy side dish to almost any main dish recipe.

- Steamed Broccoli and Carrots (page 18). I make a big batch of steamed vegetables each week and then reheat them to go with almost any main dish. Use any mix of vegetables you like, including frozen options.

- In general, when planning meals to prep ahead, remember to include a combination of protein, healthy fat, and complex carbohydrates. Use this chart as a guide for packing up portions:

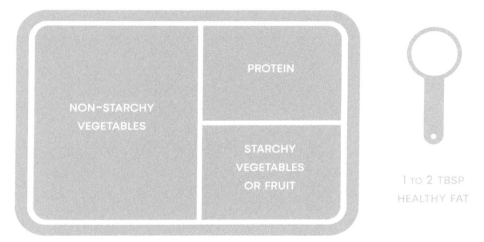

ADAPTING RECIPES FOR DIFFERENT MODELS

The recipes in this book were created using a 6-quart Instant Pot®, but most can also be made in an 8-quart model without changing ingredient quantities. I don't recommend using a 3-quart Instant Pot®, because it will be too small for most of the recipes in this book.

SCALING RECIPES UP OR DOWN

The recipes in this book were created to make a minimum of six servings. You can generally increase the serving size of any recipe up to about 25 percent, but be careful not to fill your Instant Pot® past the max line marked on the stainless steel pot. If you need to scale down, most recipes can be cut in half; just be sure to use a minimum of 1 cup of liquid.

Stocking Your Kitchen

There are some Instant Pot® accessories I find useful when cooking. I also keep a well-stocked pantry for ingredients I use often when meal prepping. It's one more way to keep my meal prep efficient and focused—no last-minute surprises. Set yourself up for success by stocking your kitchen and pantry with the following essentials.

RECOMMENDED KITCHEN EQUIPMENT

The Instant Pot® is pretty amazing on its own, but these extra pieces of equipment can help take it to the next level:

Ceramic or glass baking dish: For pot-in-pot cooking, a 7- or 8-inch, 2-quart ceramic or glass baking dish works well. Make sure it's oven-proof and can withstand pressure cooking.

Cutting boards: I have a bamboo cutting board for vegetables and a couple of dishwasher-safe plastic cutting boards for prepping raw meat and poultry.

Fine-mesh strainer: I use my strainer for rinsing rice or quinoa before cooking.

Immersion blender: Perfect for blending soups right in the pot.

Sharp knives: I recommend having at least one large chef's knife and one small paring knife for prepping ingredients.

Stainless-steel steamer basket: This basket fits inside the inner pot and has many great uses, including steaming vegetables and hard-boiling eggs. Look for one that is intended for use with a 6-quart Instant Pot®.

Utensils: A wooden spoon, spatula, ladle, and tongs are my go-tos. I like to buy wooden, silicone, or stainless steel ones that can be washed in the dishwasher and handle heavy use.

RECOMMENDED PANTRY ITEMS

You can stock your healthy pantry with dry goods so you'll have what you need for months. I always have the following items on hand:

- Canned foods, including full-fat coconut milk, tomato paste, and diced tomatoes

- Cornstarch or arrowroot starch, to thicken sauces

- Dried beans, grains, legumes, and so on, including black beans, quinoa, chia seeds, white and brown rice, whole-wheat and brown rice pasta, rolled oats, and green or brown lentils

- Dried herbs and spices, such as black pepper, cayenne pepper, chili powder, ground cinnamon, curry powder, garlic powder, oregano, salt, thyme, and turmeric

- Jarred items, including balsamic vinegar, Dijon mustard, peanut butter and almond butter, Sriracha sauce, Thai green curry paste, white wine vinegar, and Worcestershire sauce

- Low-sodium broths (beef, chicken, and vegetable)

- Extra-virgin olive oil and/or coconut oil

- Reduced-sodium soy sauce (use tamari for gluten-free diets)

- Sweeteners, including honey and maple syrup

- Vanilla extract

About the Recipes

There are several different recipe types you'll see in this book, all designed to add versatility and make your life easier.

Advance Prep. These recipes include ingredients that can be prepped ahead of time and stored in jars or zip-top bags for several days before cooking. When you're ready to cook, toss the ingredients into your Instant Pot®, add the necessary liquid, and set it to the appropriate pressure level and cooking time.

Freezer Friendly. These recipes freeze well after cooking. Just thaw them overnight and reheat when you're ready to serve.

One Pot. Make a whole meal in just one pot—no other equipment needed. This makes preparation and cleanup so easy.

The recipes also include nutritional information and dietary labels. Additionally, many include tips for how a recipe can be modified to meet certain dietary needs.

Dairy-Free. These recipes are free of ingredients using milk products OR offer substitutions/modifications to make the dishes dairy-free.

Gluten-Free. These recipes are free of gluten OR offer substitutions/modifications to make the dishes gluten-free.

Vegetarian. These recipes are free of meat OR offer substitutions/modifications to make the dishes vegetarian.

Vegan. These recipes are free of all animal products OR offer substitutions/modifications to make the dishes vegan.

After reading this chapter, I hope you are inspired to make super-efficient, healthy meals in your Instant Pot®. Lucky for you, simple-to-make, delicious, nutrient-packed recipes are just a few pages away. There's no better time than now to get started!

Broccoli-Cheddar Soup, page 84

Basics and Staples

STEAMED BROCCOLI AND CARROTS

SERVES 6

PREP AND FINISHING:
10 MINUTES

PRESSURE COOK:
2 MINUTES ON HIGH

RELEASE:
QUICK

TOTAL TIME:
22 MINUTES

DAIRY-FREE
GLUTEN-FREE
VEGAN

PER SERVING
Calories: 41; Fat: 0g;
Carbohydrates: 10g;
Fiber: 3g; Protein: 2g;
Sodium: 62mg

One of my most important strategies for staying healthy is to make sure I eat enough vegetables. The Instant Pot® makes this goal so easy! I buy a head of broccoli and a big bag of carrots every week so I can have steamed vegetables on hand. Whenever I need a veggie side, I reheat these on the stovetop or in the microwave and serve them with butter or coconut oil and a sprinkle of salt.

1 medium head broccoli, cut into florets (about 2 cups)
1 pound carrots, peeled and cut into 1-inch-long chunks
1 cup water

1. Place the broccoli florets and carrots in a steamer basket.

2. Pour the water into the inner pot, then set the steamer basket inside.

3. Lock the lid into place. Select Pressure Cook or Manual; set the pressure to High and the time to 2 minutes. Make sure the steam knob is in the sealed position. After cooking, quick release the pressure.

4. Unlock and remove the lid. Serve immediately.

5. If storing the vegetables for later use, remove the steamer basket and place it in the sink. Run cold water over the vegetables to cool them down. Alternatively, place the vegetables in a large bowl of ice water to cool them down quickly. Cover and refrigerate for up to 7 days.

MEAL PREP TIP: *These steamed vegetables go with so many other recipes, including Honey Sesame Chicken (page 136), Lemon-Garlic Shrimp Scampi (page 110), and Beef Burgundy (page 144). Reheat the steamed vegetables on the stovetop or in the microwave. For the microwave, place the vegetables in a microwave-safe bowl with a teaspoon of water. Cover with plastic wrap and poke a few holes in the wrap. Heat on high for 45 to 60 seconds. Serve hot.*

WHITE BASMATI RICE

SERVES 6

PREP AND FINISHING:
5 MINUTES

PRESSURE COOK:
8 MINUTES ON HIGH

RELEASE:
QUICK

TOTAL TIME:
23 MINUTES

ADVANCE PREP
DAIRY-FREE
FREEZER FRIENDLY
GLUTEN-FREE
VEGAN

PER SERVING
Calories: 225; Fat: 0g;
Carbohydrates: 49g;
Fiber: 1g; Protein: 4g;
Sodium: 3mg

I gave away my rice cooker after I had so much success making rice in the Instant Pot®. Not only is it faster than using the rice cooker, but the end result is fluffier rice. I make a batch every week and serve it with almost any main dish. For a treat, I make super-quick rice pudding by reheating the rice with some milk, butter, cinnamon, raisins, and maple syrup. You can also blend cooked rice with water and then strain it to make homemade rice milk.

2 cups white basmati rice, rinsed
3 cups water

1. Combine the rice and water in the inner pot.

2. Lock the lid into place. Select Pressure Cook or Manual; set the pressure to High and the time to 8 minutes. Make sure the steam release knob is in the sealed position. After cooking, quick release the pressure.

3. Unlock and remove the lid. Serve the rice immediately, or place it in an airtight container and refrigerate for up to 5 days or freeze for up to 2 months.

ADVANCE PREP TIP: *Rinse and drain your rice and place it in the Instant Pot® with the water up to 8 hours ahead of time. When you're ready to start cooking, just plug it in and set the time.*

MEAL PREP TIP: *White rice is incredibly versatile, soaking up the flavors of whatever it is served with. Try it with Green Thai Coconut Curry with Tofu (page 90), Kung Pao Chicken (page 134), and Indian Butter Chicken (page 138). When reheating cooked rice in the microwave or on the stovetop, add about 1 teaspoon of water per serving to keep it moist and prevent it from burning.*

BROWN RICE

SERVES 8

PREP AND FINISHING:
5 MINUTES

PRESSURE COOK:
22 MINUTES ON HIGH

RELEASE:
NATURAL FOR
10 MINUTES,
THEN QUICK

TOTAL TIME:
47 MINUTES

ADVANCE PREP
DAIRY-FREE
FREEZER FRIENDLY
GLUTEN-FREE
VEGAN

PER SERVING
Calories: 171; Fat: 1g;
Carbohydrates: 36g;
Fiber: 2g; Protein: 4g;
Sodium: 3mg

Steamed brown rice can be served with just about anything. It adds a pleasant, nutty flavor to dishes. Brown rice is a must-have staple for meal planning because it reheats so well and is so versatile. Two cups of dry brown rice yields about 8 cups of cooked brown rice.

2 cups long-grain brown rice, rinsed
2½ cups water

1. Combine the brown rice and water in the inner pot.

2. Lock the lid into place. Select Pressure Cook or Manual; set the pressure to High and the time to 22 minutes. Make sure the steam release knob is in the sealed position. After cooking, naturally release the pressure for 10 minutes, then quick release any remaining pressure.

3. Unlock and remove the lid. Serve the rice immediately, or place it in an airtight container and refrigerate for up to 7 days or freeze for up to 2 months.

ADVANCE PREP TIP: *Rinse and drain your rice and place it in the Instant Pot® with the water up to 8 hours ahead of time. When ready to start cooking, just plug it in and set the time.*

MEAL PREP TIP: *This rice can go a long way over the course of a week. Try it with Lemon Piccata Chicken (page 126), Honey Sesame Chicken (page 136), and Sweet and Sour Pork (page 170). Brown rice can be reheated on the stovetop or in the microwave. To microwave, place the rice in a microwave-safe bowl with 1 teaspoon of water per serving. Cover with plastic wrap and poke a few holes in the wrap. Heat on high for 45 to 60 seconds. Serve hot.*

QUINOA

SERVES 6

PREP AND FINISHING:
5 MINUTES

PRESSURE COOK:
1 MINUTE ON HIGH

RELEASE:
NATURAL FOR
10 MINUTES,
THEN QUICK

TOTAL TIME:
26 MINUTES

DAIRY-FREE
FREEZER FRIENDLY
GLUTEN-FREE
VEGAN

PER SERVING
Calories: 209; Fat: 3g;
Carbohydrates: 36g;
Fiber: 4g; Protein: 8g;
Sodium: 3mg

If you've ever made quinoa on the stovetop, you know that it has the tendency to boil over or get overcooked. Making it in the Instant Pot® takes away all the hassle. The result is fluffy, nutty quinoa that's perfect for meal prepping.

2 cups quinoa, rinsed
2 cups water

1. Combine the quinoa and water in the inner pot.

2. Lock the lid into place. Select Pressure Cook or Manual; set the pressure to High and the time to 1 minute. Make sure the steam release knob is in the sealed position. After cooking, naturally release the pressure for 10 minutes, then quick release any remaining pressure.

3. Unlock and remove the lid. Using a fork, fluff the quinoa.

4. Serve the quinoa immediately, or place it in an airtight container and refrigerate for up to 5 days or freeze for up to 2 months.

MEAL PREP TIP: *Quinoa is an incredibly versatile ingredient and a great source of protein. You can serve it in the same way as you would rice. Try it with Sweet and Sour Brussels Sprouts (page 61) or Beef Goulash (page 100).*

INGREDIENT VARIATION: *For even more flavor, use low-sodium vegetable broth instead of water.*

LENTILS

SERVES 8

PREP AND FINISHING:
5 MINUTES

PRESSURE COOK:
20 MINUTES ON HIGH

RELEASE:
NATURAL FOR
10 MINUTES,
THEN QUICK

TOTAL TIME:
45 MINUTES

DAIRY-FREE
FREEZER FRIENDLY
GLUTEN-FREE
VEGAN

PER SERVING
Calories: 166; Fat: 1g;
Carbohydrates: 28g;
Fiber: 5g; Protein: 12g;
Sodium: 3mg

Lentils are a healthy source of plant-based protein. They make a delicious addition to just about any salad, and they're also great in soups, stews, and pasta dishes. Cooked lentils have a mild flavor and can be dressed up by stirring in ½ teaspoon of whatever seasoning you like, including curry powder, chili powder, or Italian seasoning. Make sure you wait until after cooking to season the lentils with salt or lemon juice; salt and acid can prevent the lentils from cooking properly.

2 cups dried brown or green lentils, picked through and rinsed

4 cups water

1. Combine the lentils and water in the inner pot.

2. Lock the lid into place. Select Pressure Cook or Manual; set the pressure to High and the time to 20 minutes. Make sure the steam release knob is in the sealed position. After cooking, naturally release the pressure for 10 minutes, then quick release any remaining pressure.

3. Unlock and remove the lid. Stir the lentils. Serve immediately, or place the lentils in an airtight container and refrigerate for up to 5 days or freeze for up to 2 months.

COOKING TIP: *Don't use red lentils for this recipe, as they will get too mushy. Green or brown lentils work best.*

INGREDIENT VARIATION: *For even more flavor, use low-sodium vegetable or chicken broth in place of the water.*

BLACK BEANS

SERVES 6

PREP AND FINISHING:
10 MINUTES

PRESSURE COOK:
25 MINUTES ON HIGH

RELEASE:
NATURAL FOR
10 MINUTES,
THEN QUICK

TOTAL TIME:
55 MINUTES

DAIRY-FREE
FREEZER FRIENDLY
GLUTEN-FREE
VEGAN

PER SERVING
Calories: 221; Fat: 1g;
Carbohydrates: 40g;
Fiber: 10g; Protein: 14g;
Sodium: 3mg

If you've never had black beans cooked from scratch before, you're in for a real treat. They come out perfectly tender and are so versatile—especially in tacos, soups, burrito bowls, and salads. They're also budget-friendly and a great way to add more plant-based goodness to your life.

2 cups dried black beans, rinsed and drained
2 bay leaves
8 cups water

1. Combine the black beans, bay leaves, and water in the inner pot.

2. Lock the lid into place. Select Pressure Cook or Manual; set the pressure to High and the time to 25 minutes. Make sure the steam release knob is in the sealed position. After cooking, naturally release the pressure for 10 minutes, then quick release any remaining pressure.

3. Unlock and remove the lid. Drain the beans. Discard the bay leaves.

4. Serve the beans immediately, or place them in an airtight container and refrigerate for up to 5 days or freeze for up to 2 months.

COOKING TIP: *To cut down on the cooking time, soak the beans in water at room temperature for at least 8 hours. Drain and rinse the beans, then cook on High pressure for 15 minutes.*

YUKON GOLD POTATOES

SERVES 6

PREP AND FINISHING:
10 MINUTES

PRESSURE COOK:
10 MINUTES ON HIGH

RELEASE:
NATURAL FOR
10 MINUTES,
THEN QUICK

TOTAL TIME:
40 MINUTES

DAIRY-FREE
GLUTEN-FREE
VEGAN

PER SERVING
Calories: 119; Fat: 0g;
Carbohydrates: 27g;
Fiber: 2g; Protein: 3g;
Sodium: 8mg

Cooking whole potatoes in the pressure cooker is one of my favorite tricks. You don't even have to prick the potatoes like when you're going to microwave or bake them. Just wash them and pop them onto the trivet with some water. After 10 minutes of cooking time, you have fork-tender potatoes that are the perfect side dish to serve throughout the week.

1 cup water
2 pounds Yukon Gold potatoes

1. Place the trivet in the inner pot, then pour in the water. Place the potatoes on the trivet.

2. Lock the lid into place. Select Pressure Cook or Manual; set the pressure to High and the time to 10 minutes. Make sure the steam release knob is in the sealed position. After cooking, naturally release the pressure for 10 minutes, then quick release any remaining pressure.

3. Unlock and remove the lid. Using tongs, transfer the potatoes to a serving plate or bowl. Serve immediately, or place the potatoes in an airtight container and refrigerate for up to 5 days.

INGREDIENT VARIATION: *Substitute red potatoes or new potatoes for the Yukon Gold potatoes.*

MEAL PREP TIPS: *Season with sea salt and freshly ground black pepper before serving. These potatoes can be served with many different dishes, including Hawaiian Pineapple Pork (page 164) and Beef Stroganoff with Spring Green Peas (page 146).*

SWEET POTATOES

SERVES 6

PREP AND FINISHING:
5 MINUTES

PRESSURE COOK:
15 MINUTES ON HIGH

RELEASE:
NATURAL FOR
10 MINUTES,
THEN QUICK

TOTAL TIME:
40 MINUTES

DAIRY-FREE
GLUTEN-FREE
VEGAN

PER SERVING
Calories: 112; Fat: 0g;
Carbohydrates: 26g;
Fiber: 4g; Protein: 2g;
Sodium: 72mg

Cooked sweet potatoes are a healthy meal prep staple. Make a batch on the weekend or in the middle of the week, and use them as a source of healthy carbohydrates. Sweet potatoes are naturally sweet and delicious served with butter or coconut oil and a sprinkle of sea salt. If eating the skin, I recommend purchasing organic sweet potatoes.

1 cup water
6 medium sweet potatoes

1. Place a trivet or steaming rack inside the inner pot, then pour in the water. Arrange the sweet potatoes on the rack.

2. Lock the lid into place. Select Pressure Cook or Manual; set the pressure to High and the time to 15 minutes. Make sure the steam release knob is in the sealed position. After cooking, naturally release the pressure for 10 minutes, then quick release any remaining pressure.

3. Unlock and remove the lid. Serve the sweet potatoes immediately, or place them in an airtight container and refrigerate for up to 5 days.

MEAL PREP TIP: *Try these sweet potatoes with Sweet and Sour Brussels Sprouts (page 61) or Sloppy Joes (page 152). To reheat the sweet potatoes, place them in a microwave-safe bowl with 1 teaspoon of water. Cover with plastic wrap and poke a few holes in the wrap. Microwave on high for 45 to 60 seconds. Serve hot.*

HARD-BOILED EGGS

SERVES 6

PREP AND FINISHING:
5 MINUTES

PRESSURE COOK:
7 MINUTES ON HIGH

RELEASE:
NATURAL FOR
5 MINUTES,
THEN QUICK

TOTAL TIME:
27 MINUTES

DAIRY-FREE
GLUTEN-FREE
ONE POT
VEGETARIAN

PER SERVING
Calories: 71; Fat: 5g;
Carbohydrates: 0g;
Fiber: 0g; Protein: 6g;
Sodium: 70mg

When you make hard-boiled eggs in the Instant Pot®, they are perfectly cooked and easy to peel. What could be better? I like to make a half dozen at a time and enjoy them as snacks throughout the week.

1 cup water
6 eggs

1. Place the trivet in the inner pot, then pour in the water. Arrange the eggs on the trivet.

2. Lock the lid into place. Select Pressure Cook or Manual; set the pressure to High and the time to 7 minutes. Make sure the steam release knob is in the sealed position. After cooking, naturally release the pressure for 5 minutes, then quick release any remaining pressure.

3. Unlock and remove the lid. Using tongs or a serving spoon, transfer the eggs to a bowl and run them under cool tap water to stop the cooking process.

4. Peel the eggs and enjoy, or leave them unpeeled and store them in an airtight container in the refrigerator for up to 1 week.

COOKING TIP: *You can cook as few as two and as many as eight large eggs in a 6-quart Instant Pot® at the same time.*

WHOLE COOKED CHICKEN

SERVES 10

PREP AND FINISHING:
10 MINUTES

PRESSURE COOK:
30 MINUTES ON HIGH

RELEASE:
NATURAL FOR
10 MINUTES,
THEN QUICK

TOTAL TIME:
60 MINUTES

DAIRY-FREE
FREEZER FRIENDLY
GLUTEN-FREE

PER SERVING
Calories: 128; Fat: 4g;
Carbohydrates: 0g;
Fiber: 0g; Protein: 21g;
Sodium: 423mg

You'll never believe how easy it is to cook a whole chicken in the Instant Pot®. I usually make at least one a week as part of my healthy meal prep. I use the cooked chicken in salads and sandwiches, or reheated with rice and veggies. Cooked chicken also freezes very well; just remove the bones and skins before storing the meat.

1 cup water
1 (4½- to 5-pound) whole chicken, giblets removed
1 tablespoon extra-virgin olive oil
1 teaspoon dried thyme
½ teaspoon garlic powder
2 teaspoons fine sea salt

1. Place the trivet in the inner pot, then pour in the water. Place the chicken breast-side down on the trivet and drizzle it with the olive oil. Sprinkle the thyme, garlic powder, and salt over the chicken.

2. Lock the lid into place. Select Pressure Cook or Manual; set the pressure to High and the time to 30 minutes. Make sure the steam release knob is in the sealed position. After cooking, naturally release the pressure for 10 minutes, then quick release any remaining pressure.

3. Unlock and remove the lid. Using tongs, transfer the chicken to a serving plate.

4. Serve immediately, or place the chicken in an airtight container and refrigerate for up to 4 days or freeze for up to 2 months.

MEAL PREP TIP: For brown, crispy chicken skin, after the cooking is complete, transfer the whole chicken to a baking sheet, breast-side up, and place it under the broiler for several minutes until the skin browns to your liking.

Coconut Blueberry Chia Pudding, page 39

3

Breakfast and Brunch

CINNAMON-APPLE STEEL-CUT OATS

SERVES 8

PREP AND FINISHING:
10 MINUTES

SAUTÉ:
5 MINUTES

PRESSURE COOK:
8 MINUTES ON HIGH

RELEASE:
NATURAL FOR
10 MINUTES,
THEN QUICK

TOTAL TIME:
43 MINUTES

DAIRY-FREE (SEE TIP)
FREEZER FRIENDLY
GLUTEN-FREE (SEE TIP)
ONE POT
VEGAN (SEE TIP)

PER SERVING
Calories: 123; Fat: 2g;
Carbohydrates: 25g;
Fiber: 3g; Protein: 2g;
Sodium: 12mg

Cooking steel-cut oats on the stovetop always seems to take forever, and who has that kind of time in the morning? The oats in this Instant Pot® version turn out perfectly cooked, creamy, and full of sweet cinnamon-apple flavor—no stirring required. It's the perfect healthy way to start the day.

1 tablespoon unsalted butter
2 red apples, cored and chopped
1 tablespoon ground cinnamon
2 cups uncooked steel-cut oats
3⅓ cups water
¼ cup raisins
¼ cup pure maple syrup

1. Select Sauté and place the butter in the inner pot. Once the butter is melted, add the apples and cinnamon and cook for 2 minutes, stirring occasionally.

2. Press Cancel. Add the oats, water, and raisins to the pot. Stir to combine.

3. Lock the lid into place. Select Pressure Cook or Manual; set the pressure to High and the time to 8 minutes. Make sure the steam release knob is in the sealed position.

4. After cooking, naturally release the pressure for 10 minutes, then quick release any remaining pressure.

5. Unlock and remove the lid. Stir in the maple syrup.

6. Serve immediately, or place the oatmeal in an airtight container and refrigerate for up to 4 days or freeze for up to 2 months.

DAIRY-FREE & VEGAN OPTION: *Use coconut oil instead of butter.*

GLUTEN-FREE OPTION: *Use certified gluten-free oats to make this dish*

MEAL PREP TIP: *The cooked oats reheat nicely in the microwave. Place each serving in a microwave-safe bowl with 1 teaspoon of water. Cover with plastic wrap and poke a few holes in the wrap. Heat on high for 45 to 60 seconds. Serve hot.*

PUMPKIN SPICE OATMEAL

SERVES 6

PREP AND FINISHING:
10 MINUTES

PRESSURE COOK:
3 MINUTES ON HIGH

RELEASE:
QUICK

TOTAL TIME:
23 MINUTES

DAIRY-FREE (SEE TIP)
GLUTEN-FREE (SEE TIP)
ONE POT
VEGAN (SEE TIP)

PER SERVING
Calories: 169; Fat: 4g;
Carbohydrates: 26g;
Fiber: 2g; Protein: 8g;
Sodium: 141mg

This oatmeal dish is ridiculously easy and makes your kitchen smell heavenly. It's a bowl of warmth and comfort to start your day. The pumpkin purée adds nutrition and makes your oatmeal taste like a pumpkin pie.

4 cups low-fat milk
2 cups rolled oats
½ cup pumpkin purée
1 teaspoon pure vanilla extract
½ teaspoon ground cinnamon
⅛ teaspoon fine sea salt
¼ cup pure maple syrup
¼ cup chopped unsalted almonds

1. Combine the milk, oats, pumpkin, vanilla extract, cinnamon, and salt in the inner pot. Mix well.

2. Lock the lid into place. Select Pressure Cook or Manual; set the pressure to High and the time to 3 minutes. Make sure the steam release knob is in the sealed position. After cooking, quick release the pressure.

3. Unlock and remove the lid. Stir in the maple syrup and almonds.

4. Serve immediately, or place the oatmeal in an airtight container and refrigerate for up to 4 days.

COOKING TIP: *Be sure to use regular rolled oats, not quick-cooking oats.*

DAIRY-FREE & VEGAN OPTION: *Use unsweetened almond milk instead of low-fat regular milk.*

GLUTEN-FREE OPTION: *Use certified gluten-free oats to make this dish gluten-free.*

CHOCOLATE-BANANA QUINOA BREAKFAST BOWLS

SERVES 6

PREP AND FINISHING:
10 MINUTES

PRESSURE COOK:
12 MINUTES ON LOW

RELEASE:
NATURAL FOR
10 MINUTES,
THEN QUICK

TOTAL TIME:
42 MINUTES

DAIRY-FREE
GLUTEN-FREE
VEGAN

PER SERVING
Calories: 414; Fat: 22g;
Carbohydrates: 50g;
Fiber: 6g; Protein: 8g;
Sodium: 94mg

Quinoa is an ideal breakfast food because of its protein content and soft, fluffy texture. The banana and maple syrup in this recipe add just enough sweetness, and the cocoa powder and coconut milk make this a delicious, decadent way to start the day.

1½ cups quinoa, rinsed

2 medium ripe bananas, peeled and chopped

1 (15-ounce) can full-fat coconut milk

1½ cups water

1 teaspoon pure vanilla extract

1 tablespoon unsweetened cocoa powder

¼ teaspoon fine sea salt

¼ cup pure maple syrup

1. Place the quinoa in the inner pot and add the bananas, coconut milk, water, vanilla extract, and cocoa powder. Stir to combine.

2. Lock the lid into place. Select Pressure Cook or Manual; set the pressure to Low and the time to 12 minutes. Make sure the steam release knob is in the sealed position. After cooking, naturally release the pressure for 10 minutes, then quick release any remaining pressure.

3. Unlock and remove the lid. Stir in the salt and maple syrup.

4. Serve immediately, or place the quinoa in single-serving airtight containers and refrigerate for up to 4 days.

GRAIN-FREE BIRCHER BOWLS WITH YOGURT

SERVES 8

PREP AND FINISHING:
10 MINUTES

PRESSURE COOK:
3 MINUTES ON HIGH

RELEASE:
QUICK

TOTAL TIME:
23 MINUTES

DAIRY-FREE (SEE TIP)
GLUTEN-FREE
ONE POT
VEGAN (SEE TIP)

PER SERVING
Calories: 293; Fat: 7g;
Carbohydrates: 48g;
Fiber: 4g; Protein: 10g;
Sodium: 99mg

A Bircher bowl is a traditional Swiss breakfast made by soaking oats in milk and serving them with fresh fruit. This version is made grain-free using nuts and seeds for a super-healthy blend of fiber and nutrients. The mixture is cooked briefly in the Instant Pot®, which transforms it into a hot porridge that gets served with protein-rich low-fat yogurt for an energizing start to the day.

¼ cup unsalted pumpkin seeds
¼ cup unsalted sunflower seeds
¼ cup chia seeds
2 apples, cored and chopped into bite-size pieces
1 cup low-fat milk
1 teaspoon pure vanilla extract
½ teaspoon ground cinnamon
1 cup pure maple syrup
1 (32-ounce) container low-fat plain yogurt

1. Combine the pumpkin seeds, sunflower seeds, chia seeds, apples, milk, vanilla extract, and cinnamon in the inner pot. Stir to combine.

2. Lock the lid into place. Select Pressure Cook or Manual; set the pressure to High and the time to 3 minutes. Make sure the steam release knob is in the sealed position. After cooking, quick release the pressure.

GRAIN-FREE BIRCHER BOWLS WITH YOGURT *continues*

3. Unlock and remove the lid. Stir in the maple syrup.

4. Serve the warm seed mixture over the yogurt in individual bowls, or place it in an airtight container and refrigerate for up to 4 days.

INGREDIENT VARIATION: *You can use whatever chopped nuts or seeds you like or have on hand.*

DAIRY-FREE & VEGAN OPTION: *Use unsweetened almond milk instead of low-fat regular milk. Use dairy-free plain yogurt instead of dairy yogurt.*

COCONUT-BLUEBERRY CHIA PUDDING

SERVES 8

PREP AND FINISHING:
10 MINUTES

PRESSURE COOK:
3 MINUTES ON HIGH

RELEASE:
NATURAL FOR
5 MINUTES,
THEN QUICK

TOTAL TIME:
28 MINUTES, PLUS
1 HOUR TO CHILL

DAIRY-FREE
GLUTEN-FREE (SEE TIP)
ONE POT
VEGAN

PER SERVING
Calories: 390; Fat: 24g;
Carbohydrates: 42g;
Fiber: 13g; Protein: 8g;
Sodium: 16mg

Chia seeds are high in fiber, protein, and omega-3 fatty acids, and they're the perfect ingredient for a healthy breakfast pudding. The combination of chia seeds and oats also makes for a great chewy texture. I like this with blueberries because they're not too tart, but you can use your favorite frozen berry instead, if you like.

1 (14-ounce) can full-fat coconut milk
1 cup water
1 (12-ounce) bag frozen blueberries
1 cup chia seeds
1 cup rolled oats
½ cup pure maple syrup
½ teaspoon pure vanilla extract
Fresh berries, for garnish (optional)

1. Combine the coconut milk, water, blueberries, chia seeds, oats, maple syrup, and vanilla extract in the inner pot.

COCONUT-BLUEBERRY CHIA PUDDING *continues*

2. Lock the lid into place. Select Pressure Cook or Manual; set the pressure to High and the time to 3 minutes. Make sure the steam release knob is in the sealed position. After cooking, naturally release the pressure for 5 minutes, then quick release any remaining pressure.

3. Unlock and remove the lid. Pour the pudding into individual serving cups and refrigerate until it sets, about 1 hour. Serve cold garnished with berries, or cover tightly and refrigerate for up to 4 days.

COOKING TIP: *Because of the time needed for the pudding to set, this recipe is ideal for making the day before serving.*

GLUTEN-FREE OPTION: *Use certified gluten-free oats to make this dish gluten-free.*

SPICY SAUSAGE AND POTATO HASH

SERVES 6

PREP AND FINISHING:
10 MINUTES

SAUTÉ:
5 MINUTES

PRESSURE COOK:
10 MINUTES ON HIGH

RELEASE:
NATURAL FOR
10 MINUTES,
THEN QUICK

TOTAL TIME:
45 MINUTES

ADVANCE PREP
DAIRY-FREE
GLUTEN-FREE
ONE POT

PER SERVING
Calories: 306; Fat: 10g;
Carbohydrates: 37g;
Fiber: 6g; Protein: 18g;
Sodium: 459mg

This savory breakfast dish is full of spicy protein and hearty white potatoes. It's nice enough to serve for a Sunday brunch, yet fast enough to make on a weekday morning. Serve it with a piping hot cup of coffee and you'll be set for a productive day.

1 tablespoon extra-virgin olive oil

1 pound uncooked chorizo, sliced into ¾-inch-thick pieces

2 garlic cloves, minced

1 yellow onion, diced

½ teaspoon dried rosemary

1 cup low-sodium chicken broth

6 medium white potatoes, peeled and cut into bite-size pieces

½ teaspoon freshly ground black pepper

1 tablespoon balsamic vinegar

1. Select Sauté and add the olive oil to the inner pot. Once the oil is hot, add the chorizo, garlic, onion, and rosemary. Sauté for 3 minutes, stirring occasionally.

2. Press Cancel, then pour the broth into the pot. Use a wooden spoon to scrape up any pieces of food stuck to the bottom of the pot. Add the potatoes to the pot and stir to combine.

SPICY SAUSAGE AND POTATO HASH *continues*

3. Lock the lid into place. Select Pressure Cook or Manual; set the pressure to High and the time to 10 minutes. Make sure the steam release knob is in the sealed position. After cooking, naturally release the pressure for 10 minutes, then quick release any remaining pressure.

4. Unlock and remove the lid. Stir in the black pepper and vinegar.

5. Serve immediately, or place the hash in an airtight container and refrigerate for up to 4 days.

ADVANCE PREP TIP: *Slice the sausage and chop the garlic and onion up to 2 days ahead of time. Store the prepped ingredients in an airtight container in the refrigerator until you're ready to make this dish.*

BROCCOLI AND CHEDDAR CRUSTLESS QUICHE

SERVES 6

PREP AND FINISHING:
10 MINUTES

PRESSURE COOK:
30 MINUTES ON HIGH

RELEASE:
NATURAL FOR
10 MINUTES,
THEN QUICK

TOTAL TIME:
60 MINUTES

**ONE POT
VEGETARIAN**

PER SERVING
Calories: 223; Fat: 16g;
Carbohydrates: 5g;
Fiber: 1g; Protein: 16g;
Sodium: 350mg

Making a quiche in the Instant Pot® feels like a magic trick, especially when you don't want to use your oven. It's savory with just enough cheese to feel a bit decadent, so it's perfect for weekend brunch. The flour in the recipe isn't used to create a crust; rather, it gives the quiche some structure and makes it easy to slice.

Nonstick cooking spray

1 cup water

8 eggs

½ cup low-fat milk

½ cup whole-wheat flour

1 cup chopped broccoli florets

1½ cups shredded Cheddar cheese, divided

¼ teaspoon fine sea salt

¼ teaspoon freshly ground black pepper

Fresh chopped parsley, for garnish (optional)

1. Spray an 8-inch ceramic soufflé dish with the cooking spray.

2. Place the trivet in the inner pot, then pour in the water.

3. If needed, make an aluminum sling (see page 9).

4. In a large bowl, whisk together the eggs, milk, flour, broccoli, 1 cup of the cheese, and the salt and pepper.

5. Pour the mixture into the soufflé dish. Use the sling to lower the soufflé dish onto the trivet.

BROCCOLI AND CHEDDAR CRUSTLESS QUICHE *continues*

6. Lock the lid into place. Select Pressure Cook or Manual; set the pressure to High and the time to 30 minutes. Make sure the steam release knob is in the sealed position. After cooking, naturally release the pressure for 10 minutes, then quick release any remaining pressure.

7. Unlock and remove the lid. Use the sling to remove the soufflé dish.

8. Sprinkle the remaining ½ cup of cheese on top of the quiche. Using a sharp knife, slice the quiche into 6 wedges. Serve immediately garnished with fresh parsley, or place the quiche in an airtight container and refrigerate for up to 4 days.

MEAL PREP TIP: *This quiche reheats nicely in the microwave. Place it in a microwave-safe bowl with 1 teaspoon of water. Cover with plastic wrap and poke a few holes in the wrap. Heat on high for 1 minute. Serve hot.*

HAM, EGG, AND CHEESE BAKE

SERVES 6

PREP AND FINISHING:
10 MINUTES

PRESSURE COOK:
30 MINUTES ON HIGH

RELEASE:
NATURAL FOR
10 MINUTES,
THEN QUICK

TOTAL TIME:
60 MINUTES

ADVANCE PREP
GLUTEN-FREE (SEE TIP)
ONE POT

PER SERVING
Calories: 210; Fat: 14g;
Carbohydrates: 3g;
Fiber: 0g; Protein: 17g;
Sodium: 614mg

This breakfast casserole is made using the pot-in-pot method. I recommend using a 7- or 8-inch soufflé dish. You'll love the traditional flavors of this ham, egg, and cheese dish. When it's done baking, divide the casserole among individual meal prep containers for an easy grab-and-go breakfast option that you can reheat at the office.

Nonstick cooking spray
1 cup water
8 eggs
1 cup chopped ham (about ⅓ pound)
½ cup low-fat milk
1 cup shredded Cheddar cheese, divided
¼ teaspoon fine sea salt
¼ teaspoon freshly ground black pepper

1. Spray an 8-inch ceramic soufflé dish with the cooking spray.

2. Place the trivet in the inner pot, then pour in the water.

3. If needed, make an aluminum sling (see page 9).

4. In a large bowl, whisk together the eggs, ham, milk, ½ cup of the cheese, and the salt and pepper.

5. Pour the mixture into the soufflé dish. Use the sling to lower the soufflé dish onto the trivet.

6. Lock the lid into place. Select Pressure Cook or Manual; set the pressure to High and the time to 30 minutes. Make sure the steam release knob is in the sealed position. After cooking, naturally release the pressure for 10 minutes, then quick release any remaining pressure.

7. Unlock and remove the lid. Use the sling to remove the soufflé dish.

8. Sprinkle the remaining ½ cup of cheese on top of the casserole. Using a sharp knife, slice the casserole into wedges. Serve immediately, or place in an airtight container and refrigerate for up to 4 days.

ADVANCE PREP TIP: *Follow this recipe through step 4, then pour the mixture into the soufflé dish, cover tightly with plastic wrap, and refrigerate for up to 2 days before cooking.*

GLUTEN-FREE OPTION: *Make sure the ham is gluten-free. Some is processed with gluten products.*

Vegetable Quinoa Tabbouleh, page 50

4

Grains, Beans, and Veggies

VEGETABLE QUINOA TABBOULEH

SERVES 6

PREP AND FINISHING:
10 MINUTES

PRESSURE COOK:
20 MINUTES ON HIGH

RELEASE:
QUICK

TOTAL TIME:
40 MINUTES

DAIRY-FREE
GLUTEN-FREE
VEGAN

PER SERVING
Calories: 301; Fat: 11g;
Carbohydrates: 42g;
Fiber: 6g; Protein: 10g;
Sodium: 11mg

MEAL PREP TIP:
*The sky's the limit
for other items
to include in
this salad. I like
shredded chicken,
sliced avocado,
dried cranberries,
raisins, chopped
pistachios, or Par-
mesan cheese.*

This recipe is so easy that I can practically make it in my sleep. I like to whip it up when I need something to eat on the go that doesn't have to be reheated. The cooked quinoa is fluffy and full of chewy texture, and it goes so well with the bright flavors of fresh lemon juice and herbs.

2 cups quinoa, rinsed

3½ cups water

1 tablespoon extra-virgin olive oil

Juice of 1 lemon

1 English cucumber, peeled and diced

2 medium tomatoes, diced

4 scallions, white and light green parts only, chopped

¼ cup chopped fresh flat-leaf parsley

2 tablespoons chopped fresh mint

⅓ cup pine nuts, toasted

1. Combine the quinoa, water, olive oil, and lemon juice in the inner pot.

2. Lock the lid into place. Select Pressure Cook or Manual; set the pressure to High and the time to 20 minutes. Make sure the steam release knob is in the sealed position. After cooking, quick release the pressure.

3. Unlock and remove the lid. Using a fork, fluff the quinoa, then stir in the cucumber, tomatoes, scallions, parsley, mint, and pine nuts.

4. Serve immediately, or place the tabbouleh in an airtight container and refrigerate for up to 4 days.

SPANISH RICE

SERVES 8

PREP AND FINISHING:
5 MINUTES

SAUTÉ:
5 MINUTES

PRESSURE COOK:
8 MINUTES ON HIGH

RELEASE:
NATURAL FOR
10 MINUTES,
THEN QUICK

TOTAL TIME:
38 MINUTES

DAIRY-FREE
FREEZER FRIENDLY
GLUTEN-FREE (SEE TIP)
VEGAN

PER SERVING
Calories: 218; Fat: 4g;
Carbohydrates: 41g;
Fiber: 1g; Protein: 5g;
Sodium: 152mg

My husband fondly remembers his mom making Spanish rice when he was a kid, and it's still one of his favorites. Contrary to its name, it isn't actually a Spanish dish. It is an American favorite that adds a tomato flavor punch to plain rice. The onion and bell pepper add great texture, and there's just a little bit of heat from the chili powder. I like to serve this rice with Mexican and Tex-Mex dishes.

2 tablespoons extra-virgin olive oil

1 medium yellow onion, diced

1 red bell pepper, seeded and chopped

½ teaspoon chili powder

½ teaspoon fine sea salt

2 tablespoons tomato paste

2 cups long-grain white rice, rinsed

3 cups low-sodium vegetable broth

1. Select Sauté and add the olive oil to the inner pot. Once the oil is hot, add the onion and bell pepper and sauté for 2 minutes. Add the chili powder, salt, and tomato paste. Using a wooden spoon, scrape up any browned bits stuck to the bottom of the pot.

2. Press Cancel. Add the rice and broth to the pot. Stir to combine.

SPANISH RICE *continues*

3. Lock the lid into place. Select Pressure Cook or Manual; set the pressure to High and the time to 8 minutes. Make sure the steam release knob is in the sealed position. After cooking, naturally release the pressure for 10 minutes, then quick release any remaining pressure.

4. Unlock and remove the lid. Serve immediately, or place the rice in an airtight container and refrigerate for up to 4 days or freeze for up to 2 months.

MEAL PREP TIP: *Spanish rice is a great accompaniment to many dishes, including Easy Chicken Fajitas (page 128), Pork Carnitas (page 168), and Barbacoa Beef (page 148). The rice can be reheated on the stovetop or in the microwave. To microwave it, place the rice in a microwave-safe bowl with 1 teaspoon of water. Cover with plastic wrap and poke a few holes in the wrap. Heat on high for 45 to 60 seconds. Serve hot.*

GLUTEN-FREE OPTION: *Make sure the vegetable broth is gluten-free. Some broths are made using gluten products.*

YELLOW RICE WITH PEAS AND CORN

SERVES 6

PREP AND FINISHING:
10 MINUTES

SAUTÉ:
5 MINUTES

PRESSURE COOK:
4 MINUTES ON HIGH

RELEASE:
NATURAL FOR
10 MINUTES,
THEN QUICK

TOTAL TIME:
39 MINUTES

DAIRY-FREE
FREEZER FRIENDLY
GLUTEN-FREE (SEE TIP)
VEGAN

PER SERVING
Calories: 282; Fat: 3g;
Carbohydrates: 58g;
Fiber: 3g; Protein: 8g;
Sodium: 203mg

This rice dish is a surprising win in the "easy week-night side dish" category. It goes great with almost any main dish and is full of flavor and texture. The turmeric adds lovely color, mild flavor, and natural anti-inflammatory properties.

1 tablespoon extra-virgin olive oil

2 garlic cloves, minced

1 medium yellow onion, diced

½ teaspoon ground turmeric

½ teaspoon fine sea salt

½ teaspoon freshly ground black pepper

2¼ cups low-sodium vegetable broth

2 cups white basmati rice, rinsed

1 cup frozen peas

1 cup frozen corn kernels

1. Select Sauté and add the olive oil to the inner pot. Once the oil is hot, add the garlic, onion, turmeric, salt, and pepper and sauté for 3 minutes, stirring occasionally.

2. Press Cancel and pour the broth into the pot. Using a wooden spoon, scrape up any browned bits stuck to the bottom of the pot. Add the rice, peas, and corn and stir to combine.

YELLOW RICE WITH PEAS AND CORN *continues*

3. Lock the lid into place. Select Pressure Cook or Manual; set the pressure to High and the time to 4 minutes. Make sure the steam release knob is in the sealed position. After cooking, naturally release the pressure for 10 minutes, then quick release any remaining pressure.

4. Unlock and remove the lid. Serve immediately, or place the rice in an airtight container and refrigerate for up to 4 days or freeze for up to 2 months.

MEAL PREP TIP: *Serve this recipe as a main dish with a fried egg on top.*

GLUTEN-FREE OPTION: *Make sure the vegetable broth is gluten-free. Some broths are made using gluten products.*

GREEN PEA AND PARMESAN RISOTTO

SERVES 6

PREP AND FINISHING:
10 MINUTES

SAUTÉ:
5 MINUTES

PRESSURE COOK:
5 MINUTES ON HIGH

RELEASE:
NATURAL FOR
5 MINUTES,
THEN QUICK

TOTAL TIME:
35 MINUTES

GLUTEN-FREE (SEE TIP)
VEGETARIAN

PER SERVING
Calories: 363; Fat: 10g;
Carbohydrates: 54g;
Fiber: 5g; Protein: 17g;
Sodium: 227mg

If you've ever made risotto on the stovetop, you know how much constant stirring you have to do. This recipe takes away all that work, and the result is absolutely fantastic. The risotto is creamy and rich, with a cheesy flavor and tender green peas.

2 tablespoons extra-virgin olive oil

1 medium yellow onion, diced

2 garlic cloves, minced

4 cups low-sodium vegetable broth

2 cups short-grain Arborio white rice (see Cooking Tip)

1 (16-ounce) bag frozen green peas

1 cup grated Parmesan cheese

1. Select Sauté and add the olive oil to the inner pot. Once the oil is hot, add the onion and garlic and cook for 3 minutes or until they start to soften.

2. Press Cancel and pour in the broth. Using a wooden spoon, scrape up any browned bits stuck to the bottom of the pot. Add the rice and peas and stir to combine.

GREEN PEA AND PARMESAN RISOTTO *continues*

3. Lock the lid into place. Select Pressure Cook or Manual; set the pressure to High and the time to 5 minutes. Make sure the steam release knob is in the sealed position. After cooking, naturally release the pressure for 5 minutes, then quick release any remaining pressure.

4. Unlock and remove the lid. Stir in the Parmesan cheese.

5. Serve immediately, or place the risotto in an airtight container and refrigerate for up to 4 days.

COOKING TIP: *Don't rinse the rice before using it, as this reduces the starch needed to thicken the risotto.*

GLUTEN-FREE OPTION: *Make sure the vegetable broth is gluten-free. Some broths are made using gluten products.*

MANGO STICKY BROWN RICE

SERVES 8

PREP AND FINISHING:
10 MINUTES

PRESSURE COOK:
22 MINUTES ON HIGH

RELEASE:
NATURAL FOR
10 MINUTES,
THEN QUICK

TOTAL TIME:
52 MINUTES

DAIRY-FREE
GLUTEN-FREE
VEGAN

PER SERVING
Calories: 316; Fat: 13g;
Carbohydrates: 47g;
Fiber: 3g; Protein: 5g;
Sodium: 10mg

If you have a sweet tooth like me, then you'll love serving this mango sticky rice alongside savory protein dishes like cooked chicken or fish. Or serve it on its own for breakfast. Or dessert. Any way you serve it, you'll love the subtle sweetness, warming spices, and creamy coconut flavor.

2 cups long-grain brown rice (see Cooking Tip)
1 (13.5-ounce) can light coconut milk
1 cup water
¼ teaspoon ground cardamom
½ teaspoon ground cinnamon
2 cups frozen mango chunks
2 tablespoons brown sugar

1. Place the rice, coconut milk, water, cardamom, cinnamon, and mango in the inner pot. Stir to combine.

2. Lock the lid into place. Select Pressure Cook or Manual; set the pressure to High and the time to 22 minutes. Make sure the steam release knob is in the sealed position. After cooking, naturally release the pressure for 10 minutes, then quick release any remaining pressure.

MANGO STICKY BROWN RICE *continues*

3. Unlock and remove the lid. Stir in the brown sugar.

4. Serve immediately, or place the rice in an airtight container and refrigerate for up to 4 days.

COOKING TIP: *Don't rinse the rice before using it, as this reduces the starch that helps make the rice sticky.*

INGREDIENT VARIATION: *If you don't have ground cardamom, you can just leave it out.*

MEXICAN REFRIED BEANS

SERVES 6

PREP AND FINISHING:
10 MINUTES

SAUTÉ:
5 MINUTES

PRESSURE COOK:
30 MINUTES ON HIGH

RELEASE:
NATURAL FOR
15 MINUTES,
THEN QUICK

TOTAL TIME:
1 HOUR, 10 MINUTES

DAIRY-FREE
FREEZER FRIENDLY
GLUTEN-FREE (SEE TIP)
VEGETARIAN

PER SERVING
Calories: 259; Fat: 3g;
Carbohydrates: 44g;
Fiber: 11g; Protein: 16g;
Sodium: 370mg

This Mexican-style version of refried beans is vegetarian and healthy, with no presoaking of the beans required. You'll never buy canned refried beans again. The beans are perfectly tender and seasoned and can be served as a side dish or used in dips, in wraps, or on top of nachos.

2 teaspoons extra-virgin olive oil
1 medium yellow onion, diced
2 garlic cloves, minced
1 jalapeño pepper, seeded and diced
4 cups low-sodium vegetable broth
3 cups water
2 cups dried pinto beans, rinsed and drained
1 teaspoon ground cumin
1 teaspoon dried oregano
½ teaspoon chili powder
1 teaspoon fine sea salt

1. Select Sauté and add the olive oil to the inner pot. Once the oil is hot, add the onion, garlic, and jalapeño. Sauté for 3 minutes, stirring occasionally.

2. Press Cancel and pour the broth into the pot. Using a wooden spoon, scrape up any browned bits stuck to the bottom of the pot. Add the water, beans, cumin, oregano, and chili powder and stir to combine.

MEXICAN REFRIED BEANS *continues*

3. Lock the lid into place. Select Pressure Cook or Manual; set the pressure to High and the time to 30 minutes. Make sure the steam release knob is in the sealed position. After cooking, naturally release the pressure for 15 minutes, then quick release any remaining pressure.

4. Unlock and remove the lid. Stir in the salt. Using an immersion blender, purée the beans.

5. Serve immediately, or place the beans in an airtight container and refrigerate for up to 4 days or freeze for up to 2 months.

INGREDIENT TIP: *If you don't like spicy foods, omit the jalapeño pepper.*

GLUTEN-FREE OPTION: *Make sure the vegetable broth is gluten-free. Some broths are made using gluten products.*

SWEET AND SOUR BRUSSELS SPROUTS

SERVES 6

PREP AND FINISHING:
10 MINUTES

SAUTÉ:
5 MINUTES

PRESSURE COOK:
3 MINUTES ON HIGH

RELEASE:
QUICK

TOTAL TIME:
28 MINUTES

DAIRY-FREE
GLUTEN-FREE (SEE TIP)
VEGAN

PER SERVING
Calories: 94; Fat: 4g;
Carbohydrates: 13g;
Fiber: 3g; Protein: 4g;
Sodium: 229mg

You've never had steamed Brussels sprouts like these before. They're fork-tender and covered in a tangy sweet sauce that makes for a party in your mouth. The sliced almonds add a nice bit of crunch to this delicious and healthy side dish.

2 garlic cloves, minced

⅔ cup freshly squeezed orange juice

2 tablespoons reduced-sodium soy sauce

1 tablespoon brown sugar

1 tablespoon apple cider vinegar

1 teaspoon Dijon mustard

1 tablespoon extra-virgin olive oil

1 pound Brussels sprouts, trimmed and halved

3 tablespoons unsalted sliced almonds

1. To make the sauce, place the garlic, orange juice, soy sauce, brown sugar, vinegar, and mustard in a medium bowl. Whisk to combine.

2. Select Sauté and add the oil to the inner pot. Once the oil is hot, add the Brussels sprouts and sauté for 3 minutes, stirring occasionally.

3. Press Cancel. Pour the sauce into the pot. Stir to coat the Brussels sprouts in the sauce.

SWEET AND SOUR BRUSSELS SPROUTS *continues*

4. Lock the lid into place. Select Pressure Cook or Manual; set the pressure to High and the time to 3 minutes (for firmer sprouts, set the time for 2 minutes). Make sure the steam release knob is in the sealed position. After cooking, quick release the pressure.

5. Unlock and remove the lid. Using a spoon, transfer the Brussels sprouts and sauce to a serving plate. Sprinkle with the sliced almonds.

6. Serve immediately, or place the Brussels sprouts in an airtight container and refrigerate for up to 4 days.

MEAL PREP TIP: *These sprouts reheat nicely in the microwave. Place them in a microwave-safe bowl with 1 teaspoon of water. Cover with plastic wrap and poke a few holes in the wrap. Heat on high for 45 to 60 seconds. Serve hot.*

GLUTEN-FREE OPTION: *Use tamari sauce in place of the soy sauce and be sure to buy gluten-free Dijon mustard.*

GREEN BEANS WITH MUSHROOMS AND BACON

SERVES 6

PREP AND FINISHING:
10 MINUTES

SAUTÉ:
8 MINUTES

PRESSURE COOK:
2 MINUTES ON HIGH

RELEASE:
QUICK

TOTAL TIME:
30 MINUTES

DAIRY-FREE
GLUTEN-FREE (SEE TIP)

PER SERVING
Calories: 104; Fat: 6g;
Carbohydrates: 7g;
Fiber: 3g; Protein: 8g;
Sodium: 311mg

These green beans taste just like the ones my grand-mother made during my childhood in the Midwest. I've made it easier and healthier than her recipe, though, adding mushrooms and using just a few slices of bacon to add a salty and smoky flavor. The green beans need only 2 minutes of cooking time at high pressure, making this recipe a snap.

4 bacon slices, chopped
1 garlic clove, minced
8 ounces button mushrooms, sliced
1 cup low-sodium vegetable broth
1 pound fresh or frozen green beans, trimmed
Juice of ½ medium lemon
1 tablespoon balsamic vinegar

1. Select Sauté and let the pot heat up for about 2 minutes. Add the bacon, garlic, and mushrooms and sauté for about 6 minutes, until the bacon starts to brown.

2. Press Cancel. Add the broth. Using a wooden spoon, scrape up any browned bits stuck to the bottom of the pot. Add the green beans to the pot.

3. Lock the lid into place. Select Pressure Cook or Manual; set the pressure to High and the time to 2 minutes (4 minutes if using frozen green beans). Make sure the steam release knob is in the sealed position. After cooking, quick release the pressure.

4. Unlock and remove the lid. Stir in the lemon juice and balsamic vinegar.

5. Serve immediately, or place the green beans in an airtight container and refrigerate for up to 4 days.

MEAL PREP TIP: *Don't skip the lemon juice in this dish. It locks in the beans' green color and adds a nice bright flavor to the dish.*

GLUTEN-FREE OPTION: *Make sure the vegetable broth is gluten-free. Some broths are made using gluten products.*

CREAMY CAULIFLOWER FAUX MASHED POTATOES

SERVES 6

PREP AND FINISHING:
10 MINUTES

PRESSURE COOK:
3 MINUTES ON HIGH

RELEASE:
QUICK

TOTAL TIME:
23 MINUTES

**ADVANCE PREP
(SEE TIP)
FREEZER FRIENDLY
GLUTEN-FREE
VEGETARIAN**

PER SERVING
Calories: 69; Fat: 4g;
Carbohydrates: 7g;
Fiber: 4g; Protein: 3g;
Sodium: 225mg

I was skeptical when someone told me that cooked cauliflower mashed with salt and butter tasted a lot like traditional mashed potatoes. But it's true! Okay, so it doesn't taste exactly the same, but it's a nice alternative, especially when you're looking for a lower-carb side dish. I always make a big batch and freeze the leftovers.

2½ cups water
1 large head cauliflower, cut into florets (about 4 cups)
2 tablespoons unsalted butter
½ teaspoon fine sea salt

1. Set a steamer basket in the inner pot. Pour in the water, then place the cauliflower florets in the steamer basket.

2. Lock the lid into place. Select Pressure Cook or Manual; set the pressure to High and the time to 3 minutes. Make sure the steam release knob is in the sealed position. After cooking, quick release the pressure.

3. Unlock and remove the lid. Using a serving spoon or ladle, transfer the cauliflower to a large bowl.

4. Add the butter and salt, and use a potato masher or spatula to mash the cauliflower and mix everything together. Serve immediately, or place the mashed cauliflower in an airtight container and refrigerate for up to 4 days or freeze for up to 2 months.

ADVANCE PREP TIP: *Prep the cauliflower ahead of time by washing it and cutting it into florets. Store the florets in an airtight container in the refrigerator for up to 3 days or in the freezer for up to 2 months.*

MASHED SWEET POTATOES

SERVES 10

PREP AND FINISHING:
10 MINUTES

PRESSURE COOK:
8 MINUTES ON HIGH

RELEASE:
NATURAL FOR
10 MINUTES,
THEN QUICK

TOTAL TIME:
38 MINUTES

DAIRY-FREE (SEE TIP)
GLUTEN-FREE
VEGAN (SEE TIP)

PER SERVING
Calories: 82; Fat: 2g;
Carbohydrates: 15g;
Fiber: 2g; Protein: 1g;
Sodium: 427mg

Cooking sweet potatoes in the Instant Pot® makes them so soft and creamy that you barely have to do any mashing at all. Not only will this dish make your kitchen smell amazing, but you'll also love its sweet, buttery flavor with just a hint of cinnamon. No wonder this recipe is still one of the most popular on my site.

5 medium sweet potatoes, peeled and cut into
 1-inch pieces
1 cup water
1 teaspoon ground cinnamon
2 tablespoons unsalted butter
1 tablespoon pure maple syrup
2 teaspoons fine sea salt

1. Place the sweet potatoes in the inner pot. Add the water and cinnamon.

2. Lock the lid into place. Select Pressure Cook or Manual; set the pressure to High and the time to 8 minutes. Make sure the steam release knob is in the sealed position. After cooking, naturally release the pressure for 10 minutes, then quick release any remaining pressure.

3. Unlock and remove the lid. Using a potato masher, mash the sweet potatoes with the remaining liquid in the pot. Once mashed, add the butter, maple syrup, and salt.

4. Stir to combine. Serve immediately, or place the mashed potatoes in an airtight container and refrigerate for up to 5 days.

MEAL PREP TIP: *These pair well with Honey Mustard Pork Tenderloin (page 166). They reheat nicely in the microwave or on the stovetop.*

DAIRY-FREE & VEGAN OPTION: *Use coconut oil instead of butter.*

VEGETABLE LO MEIN

SERVES 8

PREP AND FINISHING:
10 MINUTES

SAUTÉ:
5 MINUTES

PRESSURE COOK:
8 MINUTES ON HIGH

RELEASE:
QUICK

TOTAL TIME:
33 MINUTES

DAIRY-FREE
ONE POT
VEGAN

PER SERVING
Calories: 266; Fat: 3g;
Carbohydrates: 48g;
Fiber: 3g; Protein: 9g;
Sodium: 307mg

You'll appreciate having this delicious and easy vegetable noodle dish in your back pocket for those days when you're craving Chinese takeout. This version is healthy and quick—you can use fresh or frozen stir-fry veggies, and it can be made in about 30 minutes. The sauce is both sweet and sour and is sure to be everyone's favorite.

1 tablespoon extra-virgin olive oil
2 garlic cloves, minced
¼ cup reduced-sodium soy sauce
2 tablespoons rice vinegar
½ teaspoon ground ginger
2 tablespoons brown sugar
4 cups low-sodium vegetable broth
1 (16-ounce) package dried spaghetti pasta
1 (12-ounce) bag frozen stir-fry vegetables

1. Select Sauté and add the olive oil to the inner pot. Once the oil is hot, add the garlic and sauté for about 3 minutes, stirring occasionally.

2. Press Cancel. Using a wooden spoon, scrape up any browned bits stuck to the bottom of the pot. Add the soy sauce, rice vinegar, ginger, brown sugar, and broth to the pot. Stir to combine.

3. Break the spaghetti noodles in half and place them in the pot. Using a wooden spoon or spatula, push the noodles down and make sure they are covered with the liquid.

4. Place the frozen stir-fry vegetables on top of the noodle mixture, but don't stir.

5. Lock the lid into place. Select Pressure Cook or Manual; set the pressure to High and the time to 8 minutes. Make sure the steam release knob is in the sealed position. After cooking, quick release the pressure.

6. Unlock and remove the lid. Serve immediately, or place the lo mein in an airtight container and refrigerate for up to 4 days.

INGREDIENT VARIATION: *If you want to add protein to this dish, add 8 ounces of cubed extra-firm tofu with the frozen vegetables.*

STICKY NOODLES WITH TOFU

SERVES 8

PREP AND FINISHING:
10 MINUTES

SAUTÉ:
5 MINUTES

PRESSURE COOK:
6 MINUTES ON HIGH

RELEASE:
QUICK

TOTAL TIME:
31 MINUTES

DAIRY-FREE
GLUTEN-FREE (SEE TIP)
ONE POT
VEGAN

PER SERVING
Calories: 319; Fat: 9g;
Carbohydrates: 48g;
Fiber: 6g; Protein: 13g;
Sodium: 413mg

I'm all about clean, healthy eating. I love pasta, and when I can, I try to use pastas made from whole grains. For this recipe, I swapped out regular pasta noodles for whole wheat and used tofu for a plant-based protein source. The sauce is tangy and just a bit sweet. Don't be surprised if you make this dish over and over again—it's just that good.

2 tablespoons extra-virgin olive oil

3 garlic cloves, minced

10 ounces extra-firm tofu, cubed

⅓ cup reduced-sodium soy sauce

3 tablespoons apple cider vinegar

4 cups water

2 tablespoons brown sugar

1 (16-ounce) package dried whole-wheat spaghetti pasta

2 red bell peppers, seeded and thinly sliced

¼ cup unsalted cashews, chopped

1. Select Sauté and add the olive oil to the inner pot. Once the oil is hot, add the garlic and tofu and sauté for 2 minutes.

2. Press Cancel. Using a wooden spoon, scrape up any browned bits stuck to the bottom of the pot. Add the soy sauce, vinegar, water, and brown sugar to the pot. Stir to combine.

3. Break the spaghetti noodles in half and place them on top of the mixture—do not stir.

4. Lock the lid into place. Select Pressure Cook or Manual; set the pressure to High and the time to 6 minutes. Make sure the steam release knob is in the sealed position. After cooking, quick release the pressure.

5. Unlock and remove the lid. Stir in the bell peppers and cashews.

6. Serve immediately, or place the noodles in an airtight container and refrigerate for up to 4 days.

MEAL PREP TIP: *The noodles reheat nicely in the microwave. Place them in a microwave-safe bowl with 1 teaspoon of water. Cover with plastic wrap and poke a few holes in the wrap. Heat on high for 60 seconds. Serve hot.*

GLUTEN-FREE OPTION: *Use brown rice spaghetti noodles in place of whole-wheat spaghetti and tamari instead of soy sauce; increase the cooking time to 9 minutes.*

Sweet Potato and Ground Turkey Chili, page 104

5

Soups, Stews, and Chilis

SMOKED PAPRIKA LENTIL SOUP

SERVES 6

PREP AND FINISHING:
15 MINUTES

SAUTÉ:
5 MINUTES

PRESSURE COOK:
15 MINUTES ON HIGH

RELEASE:
NATURAL FOR
10 MINUTES,
THEN QUICK

TOTAL TIME:
55 MINUTES

**ADVANCE PREP
(SEE TIP)**
DAIRY-FREE
FREEZER FRIENDLY
GLUTEN-FREE (SEE TIP)
ONE POT
VEGAN

PER SERVING
Calories: 164; Fat: 3g;
Carbohydrates: 25g;
Fiber: 5g; Protein: 10g;
Sodium: 54mg

This lentil soup is healthy and full of flavor and chunky texture. Smoked paprika adds a deep flavor without making it overly spicy, and fresh lemon juice adds brightness to every spoonful.

1 tablespoon extra-virgin olive oil
1 cup dried brown lentils, rinsed and picked over
2 medium carrots, peeled and chopped
4 celery stalks, chopped
1 medium red onion, chopped
1 teaspoon dried thyme
1 teaspoon dried oregano
1 teaspoon smoked paprika
2 cups low-sodium vegetable broth
1 cup peeled and chopped tomatoes
¼ teaspoon fine sea salt (optional)
Juice of 2 lemons

1. Select Sauté and add the olive oil to the inner pot. Once the oil is hot, add the lentils, carrots, celery, and onion and sauté for 2 minutes. Add the thyme, oregano, and paprika.

2. Press Cancel and add the broth and tomatoes to the pot.

3. Lock the lid into place. Select Pressure Cook or Manual; set the pressure to High and the time to 15 minutes. Make sure the steam release knob is in the sealed position. After cooking, naturally release the pressure for 10 minutes, then quick release any remaining pressure.

4. Unlock and remove the lid. Stir in the salt (if using) and lemon juice. Using an immersion blender, blend the soup to your desired consistency.

5. Serve immediately, or place the soup in an airtight container and refrigerate for up to 4 days or freeze for up to 2 months.

ADVANCE PREP TIP: *Prepare the carrots, celery, and onion up to 3 days ahead of time, and store them in an airtight container in the refrigerator until you're ready to cook the soup.*

MEAL PREP TIP: *This lentil soup goes nicely with a scoop of cooked brown rice (page 22) or sweet potato (page 27).*

GLUTEN-FREE OPTION: *Make sure the vegetable broth is gluten-free. Some broths are made using gluten products.*

VEGETABLE MINESTRONE WITH PASTA

SERVES 6

PREP AND FINISHING:
10 MINUTES

SAUTÉ:
12 MINUTES

PRESSURE COOK:
5 MINUTES ON HIGH

RELEASE:
NATURAL FOR
10 MINUTES,
THEN QUICK

TOTAL TIME:
47 MINUTES

DAIRY-FREE (SEE TIP)
GLUTEN-FREE (SEE TIP)
ONE POT
VEGAN (SEE TIP)

PER SERVING
Calories: 402; Fat: 8g;
Carbohydrates: 67g;
Fiber: 15g; Protein: 21g;
Sodium: 901mg

Minestrone is a vegetable-filled soup fortified with tomatoes, beans, and pasta. It's the ultimate vegetarian comfort food. Think of a crisp day and a piping hot bowl of delight. I've included vegan and gluten-free substitutions at the end of this recipe to make it suitable for everyone.

2 tablespoons extra-virgin olive oil

1 medium yellow onion, chopped

3 garlic cloves, minced

4 carrots, peeled and sliced

2 celery stalks, sliced

6 cups low-sodium vegetable broth

1 teaspoon dried oregano

½ teaspoon dried thyme

1 teaspoon fine sea salt

½ teaspoon freshly ground black pepper

2 bay leaves

2 (15-ounce) cans red kidney beans, drained and rinsed

2 (15-ounce) cans diced tomatoes

1 (6-ounce) can tomato paste

2 cups dried whole-wheat macaroni pasta

½ cup grated Parmesan cheese

VEGETABLE MINESTRONE WITH PASTA *continues*

1. Select Sauté and add the olive oil to the inner pot. Once the oil is hot, add the onion, garlic, carrots, and celery; sauté for 3 minutes or until the vegetables start to soften.

2. Press Cancel and pour in the broth. Using a wooden spoon, scrape up any browned bits stuck to the bottom of the pot. Add the oregano, thyme, salt, pepper, and bay leaves, and stir to combine.

3. Add the beans, diced tomatoes, and tomato paste, but don't stir (this prevents the tomatoes from getting to the bottom of the pot, where they might burn).

4. Lock the lid into place. Select Pressure Cook or Manual; set the pressure to High and the time to 5 minutes. Make sure the steam release knob is in the sealed position. After cooking, naturally release the pressure for 10 minutes, then quick release any remaining pressure.

GLUTEN-FREE OPTION: *Make sure the vegetable broth is gluten-free. Some broths are made using gluten products.*

5. Unlock and remove the lid. Select Sauté. Remove and discard the bay leaves.

6. Let the soup come up to a simmer, then stir in the macaroni. Let the pasta cook for 7 minutes. Press Cancel and stir in the Parmesan cheese.

7. Serve immediately, or place the soup in an airtight container and refrigerate for up to 4 days.

DAIRY-FREE AND VEGAN OPTION: *Leave out the cheese to make this dish dairy-free and vegan.*

GLUTEN-FREE OPTION: *Use gluten-free macaroni pasta and increase the pasta cooking time to 11 minutes (or according to the cooking time on the package).*

CREAMY TOMATO SOUP

SERVES 6

PREP AND FINISHING:
10 MINUTES

SAUTÉ:
5 MINUTES

PRESSURE COOK:
5 MINUTES ON HIGH

RELEASE:
NATURAL FOR
10 MINUTES,
THEN QUICK

TOTAL TIME:
40 MINUTES

FREEZER FRIENDLY
GLUTEN-FREE
ONE POT
VEGETARIAN (SEE TIP)

PER SERVING
Calories: 137; Fat: 7g;
Carbohydrates: 13g;
Fiber: 3g; Protein: 7g;
Sodium: 364mg

Tomato soup out of a can was one of my favorite meals growing up. This homemade version is a lot healthier but still fast and easy. The yogurt and Parmesan cheese make the soup creamy without being too heavy. The rich tomato flavor makes the canned soup of my youth a distant memory.

2 tablespoons extra-virgin olive oil
1 medium yellow onion, chopped
3 garlic cloves, minced
3 (15-ounce) cans diced tomatoes
4 cups low-sodium chicken broth
1 teaspoon dried oregano
½ teaspoon red pepper flakes
1 teaspoon fine sea salt
½ teaspoon freshly ground black pepper
¼ cup low-fat plain yogurt
½ cup grated Parmesan cheese

1. Select Sauté and add the olive oil to the inner pot. Once the oil is hot, add the onion and garlic and cook for 3 minutes, until they start to soften.

2. Press Cancel and pour in the tomatoes and broth. Using a wooden spoon, scrape up any browned bits stuck to the bottom of the pot. Stir in the oregano, red pepper flakes, salt, and pepper.

3. Lock the lid into place. Select Pressure Cook or Manual; set the pressure to High and the time to 5 minutes. Make sure the steam release knob is in the sealed position. After cooking, naturally release the pressure for 10 minutes, then quick release any remaining pressure.

4. Unlock and remove the lid. Using an immersion blender, purée the soup to a smooth consistency. Stir in the yogurt and grated Parmesan cheese.

5. Serve immediately, or place the soup in an airtight container and refrigerate for up to 4 days or freeze for up to 2 months.

VEGETARIAN OPTION: *Use vegetable broth instead of chicken broth.*

BROCCOLI-CHEDDAR SOUP

SERVES 6

PREP AND FINISHING:
10 MINUTES

SAUTÉ:
5 MINUTES

PRESSURE COOK:
3 MINUTES ON HIGH

RELEASE:
NATURAL FOR
10 MINUTES,
THEN QUICK

TOTAL TIME:
38 MINUTES

GLUTEN-FREE
ONE POT
VEGETARIAN (SEE TIP)

PER SERVING
Calories: 324; Fat: 22g;
Carbohydrates: 12g;
Fiber: 2g; Protein: 20g;
Sodium: 447mg

Broccoli and Cheddar cheese go so well together—think quiche, casserole, and, of course, soup. This soup is comforting, nourishing, and full of flavor. As a bonus, it is also gluten-free and really easy to pull together. To make it even easier, you can buy bags of prewashed, pre-chopped broccoli florets, either fresh or frozen.

1 tablespoon extra-virgin olive oil

1 medium yellow onion, chopped

2 garlic cloves, minced

3 cups low-sodium chicken broth

1 pound fresh or frozen broccoli florets (about 3½ cups)

3 cups shredded Cheddar cheese

2 cups low-fat milk

1. Select Sauté and add the olive oil to the inner pot. Once the oil is hot, add the onion and garlic and sauté for about 2 minutes.

2. Press Cancel and add the broth. Using a wooden spoon, scrape up any browned bits stuck to the bottom of the pot. Add the broccoli to the pot.

3. Lock the lid into place. Select Pressure Cook or Manual; set the pressure to High and the time to 3 minutes (6 minutes if using frozen broccoli). Make sure the steam release knob is in the sealed position. After cooking, naturally release the pressure for 10 minutes, then quick release any remaining pressure.

4. Unlock and remove the lid. Select Sauté. Stir in the cheese until melted and combined. Stir in the milk.

5. Let the soup come to a gentle simmer, then press Cancel. Serve immediately, or place the soup in an airtight container and refrigerate for up to 4 days.

VEGETARIAN OPTION: *Use vegetable broth instead of chicken broth.*

POTATO-CORN CHOWDER

SERVES 6

PREP AND FINISHING:
10 MINUTES

SAUTÉ:
5 MINUTES

PRESSURE COOK:
8 MINUTES ON HIGH

RELEASE:
NATURAL FOR
10 MINUTES,
THEN QUICK

TOTAL TIME:
43 MINUTES

DAIRY-FREE
GLUTEN-FREE (SEE TIP)
VEGAN

PER SERVING
Calories: 226; Fat: 6g;
Carbohydrates: 41g;
Fiber: 5g; Protein: 6g;
Sodium: 412mg

This creamy, hearty chowder warms up the coldest day. It is a little bit sweet from the corn, and so thick and rich from the potatoes and almond milk that you'll be surprised it's vegan. True loving comfort in a bowl.

2 tablespoons cornstarch

½ cup water

2 tablespoons extra-virgin olive oil

1 medium yellow onion, diced

3 garlic cloves, minced

2 carrots, peeled and sliced

4 cups low-sodium vegetable broth

1½ pounds red potatoes, cut into 1-inch chunks

1 (16-ounce) bag frozen corn kernels

½ teaspoon dried rosemary

½ teaspoon dried thyme

1 teaspoon fine sea salt

½ teaspoon freshly ground black pepper

1 cup unsweetened almond milk

1. In a small bowl, make a cornstarch slurry by whisking together the cornstarch and water. Set aside.

2. Select Sauté and add the olive oil to the inner pot. Once the oil is hot, add the onion, garlic, and carrots and cook for 3 minutes, until the vegetables start to soften.

3. Press Cancel and pour in the broth. Using a wooden spoon, scrape up any browned bits stuck to the bottom of the pot. Add the potatoes, corn, rosemary, thyme, salt, and pepper, and stir to combine.

4. Lock the lid into place. Select Pressure Cook or Manual; set the pressure to High and the time to 8 minutes. Make sure the steam release knob is in the sealed position.

5. While the chowder is cooking, warm the almond milk on the stovetop or in the microwave. Whisk in the cornstarch slurry.

6. After pressure cooking is complete, naturally release the pressure for 10 minutes, and then quick release any remaining pressure.

7. Unlock and remove the lid. Stir in the almond milk mixture.

8. Serve immediately, or place the soup in an airtight container and refrigerate for up to 4 days.

INGREDIENT VARIATION: *You can use unsweetened soy milk instead of almond milk if you prefer.*

GLUTEN-FREE OPTION: *Make sure the vegetable broth is gluten-free. Some broths are made using gluten products.*

LOADED BAKED POTATO SOUP

SERVES 6

PREP AND FINISHING:
15 MINUTES

PRESSURE COOK:
20 MINUTES ON HIGH

RELEASE:
NATURAL FOR
5 MINUTES,
THEN QUICK

SAUTÉ:
5 MINUTES

TOTAL TIME:
55 MINUTES

**ADVANCE PREP
(SEE TIP)**
GLUTEN-FREE (SEE TIP)

PER SERVING
Calories: 358; Fat: 13g;
Carbohydrates: 44g;
Fiber: 2g; Protein: 16g;
Sodium: 552mg

If you love baked potatoes with all the fixings, then you'll certainly love this hearty, creamy soup that gets topped with crunchy bacon, scallions, and cheese. I've lightened up this dish by using low-fat milk and Greek yogurt instead of sour cream. It's healthy comfort food at its finest.

2 pounds medium russet potatoes (about 6 potatoes)

1 cup water

2 tablespoons unsalted butter

¼ cup all-purpose flour

4 cups low-fat milk

½ teaspoon fine sea salt

¼ teaspoon freshly ground black pepper

½ cup grated Cheddar cheese

½ cup low-fat Greek yogurt

3 scallions, white and light green parts only, chopped

3 bacon slices, cooked and crumbled

1. Scrub and rinse the potatoes and pat them dry with a clean cloth.

2. Place the trivet in the inner pot, then pour in the water. Place the potatoes on the trivet.

3. Lock the lid into place. Select Pressure Cook or Manual; set the pressure to High and the time to 20 minutes. Make sure the steam release knob is in the sealed position. After cooking, naturally release the pressure for 5 minutes, then quick release any remaining pressure.

4. Unlock and remove the lid. Using tongs, transfer the potatoes to a platter. Pour out the water and return the inner pot to the base.

5. Select Sauté and add the butter. Once the butter is melted, add the flour and whisk to combine. Add the milk, salt, and pepper and continue whisking until there are no lumps.

6. Once the milk starts to simmer, press Cancel. Add the potatoes. Using a potato masher, mash the potatoes into the milk.

7. Serve immediately. Top each serving with the cheese, yogurt, scallions, and crumbled bacon. Refrigerate leftovers in an airtight container for up to 4 days.

ADVANCE PREP TIP: *Get the toppings ready for this soup up to 2 days in advance. Grate the cheese and cook the bacon. Refrigerate in separate airtight containers until you're ready to cook the soup.*

GLUTEN-FREE OPTION: *Use your favorite gluten-free flour blend instead of all-purpose flour.*

GREEN THAI COCONUT CURRY WITH TOFU

SERVES 6

PREP AND FINISHING:
10 MINUTES

SAUTÉ:
5 MINUTES

PRESSURE COOK:
5 MINUTES ON HIGH

RELEASE:
NATURAL FOR
10 MINUTES,
THEN QUICK

TOTAL TIME:
40 MINUTES

**ADVANCE PREP
(SEE TIP)**
DAIRY-FREE
GLUTEN-FREE (SEE TIP)
ONE POT
VEGAN

PER SERVING
Calories: 302; Fat: 27g;
Carbohydrates: 13g;
Fiber: 3g; Protein: 8g;
Sodium: 254mg

You won't be able to resist this bowl of creamy coconut deliciousness and hearty vegetables. The green curry adds flavor without too much spice, the tofu adds protein, and the coconut milk fuses all the flavors.

2 tablespoons extra-virgin olive oil
1 medium yellow onion, chopped
3 garlic cloves, minced
1 cup low-sodium vegetable broth
1 (13.5-ounce) can full-fat coconut milk
1 medium zucchini, chopped (about 1 cup)
2 red bell peppers, seeded and sliced
10 ounces extra-firm tofu, cubed
½ teaspoon ground ginger
1 tablespoon Thai green curry paste
½ teaspoon fine sea salt
Juice of 1 lime

1. Select Sauté and add the olive oil to the inner pot. Once the oil is hot, add the onion and garlic and cook for about 3 minutes, or until the onion starts to soften.

2. Press Cancel and pour in the broth and coconut milk. Using a wooden spoon, scrape up any browned bits stuck to the bottom of the pot. Add the zucchini, bell peppers, tofu, ginger, and curry paste, and stir to combine.

3. Lock the lid into place. Select Pressure Cook or Manual; set the pressure to High and the time to 5 minutes. Make sure the steam release knob is in the sealed position. After cooking, naturally release the pressure for 10 minutes, then quick release any remaining pressure.

4. Unlock and remove the lid. Stir in the salt and lime juice.

5. Serve immediately, or place the curry in an airtight container and refrigerate for up to 4 days.

ADVANCE PREP TIP: *You can chop all the vegetables up to 3 days in advance and store them in two separate airtight containers (one for the onion and garlic, and the other for the zucchini and bell peppers) in the refrigerator.*

INGREDIENT VARIATION: *You can use whatever vegetables you have on hand in this recipe. You'll need about 3 cups of chopped or sliced vegetables in total.*

GLUTEN-FREE OPTION: *Make sure the vegetable broth is gluten-free. Some broths are made using gluten products.*

CHICKEN TORTILLA SOUP

SERVES 6

PREP AND FINISHING:
10 MINUTES

SAUTÉ:
5 MINUTES

PRESSURE COOK:
10 MINUTES ON HIGH

RELEASE:
NATURAL FOR
10 MINUTES,
THEN QUICK

TOTAL TIME:
45 MINUTES

DAIRY-FREE
FREEZER FRIENDLY
GLUTEN-FREE

PER SERVING
Calories: 212; Fat: 6g;
Carbohydrates: 37g;
Fiber: 7g; Protein: 9g;
Sodium: 126mg

I always get excited when I put this soup on my weekly meal plan. I love that it's so hearty and nourishing, with just enough spiciness to make it interesting. Best of all, it's super easy and versatile. The crispy baked tortilla strips are an ideal topping, adding crunch and texture, but you can also add shredded cheese, salsa, avocado, sour cream, or whatever toppings you like.

Nonstick cooking spray
6 corn tortillas, sliced into strips
2 tablespoons extra-virgin olive oil
1 medium yellow onion, diced
3 garlic cloves, minced
1 teaspoon chili powder
½ teaspoon ground cumin
6 cups low-sodium chicken broth
1½ pounds boneless, skinless chicken breasts (4 or 5 breasts)
1 (14.5-ounce) can black beans, drained and rinsed
1 (16-ounce) bag frozen corn kernels
Juice of 1 lime

1. Preheat the oven to 350°F. Line a baking sheet with parchment paper and spray it with the cooking spray.

2. Spread the tortillas strips on the baking sheet. Bake for 15 minutes, tossing once halfway through to prevent burning. While the tortilla strips are baking, prepare the soup.

3. Select Sauté and add the olive oil to the inner pot. Once the oil is hot, add the onion, garlic, chili powder, and cumin, and cook for about 3 minutes or until the onion starts to soften.

4. Press Cancel and pour in the broth. Using a wooden spoon, scrape up any browned bits stuck to the bottom of the pot. Add the chicken, black beans, and corn kernels, but don't stir.

5. Lock the lid into place. Select Pressure Cook or Manual; set the pressure to High and the time to 10 minutes. Make sure the steam release knob is in the sealed position. After cooking, naturally release the pressure for 10 minutes, then quick release any remaining pressure.

6. Unlock and remove the lid. Using tongs or a slotted spoon, transfer the chicken to a cutting board. Use two forks to shred the chicken. Return the shredded chicken to the pot. Stir in the lime juice.

7. Serve immediately with the baked tortilla strips on top, or place the soup in an airtight container and refrigerate for up to 4 days or freeze for up to 2 months.

INGREDIENT VARIATION: *If you don't want to make your own tortilla strips, buy a bag of corn tortilla chips and serve them on the side or crumbled on top of the soup.*

MOM'S CHICKEN NOODLE SOUP

SERVES 6

PREP AND FINISHING:
10 MINUTES

SAUTÉ:
15 MINUTES

PRESSURE COOK:
10 MINUTES ON HIGH

RELEASE:
NATURAL FOR
10 MINUTES,
THEN QUICK

TOTAL TIME:
55 MINUTES

DAIRY-FREE

ONE POT

PER SERVING
Calories: 371; Fat: 7g;
Carbohydrates: 38g;
Fiber: 2g; Protein: 42g;
Sodium: 421mg

My mom used to spend an entire day making a huge batch of chicken noodle soup that seemed to last the whole winter. Her work would have been a lot easier had she used a pressure cooker. In this recipe, the vegetables, chicken, and pasta are cooked in the same pot, making for easy cleanup. The soup has a flavorful broth with tons of nourishing vegetables and perfectly cooked chicken.

2 tablespoons extra-virgin olive oil

1 medium yellow onion, chopped

3 garlic cloves, minced

4 carrots, peeled and sliced

4 celery stalks, sliced

4 cups low-sodium vegetable broth

2 pounds boneless, skinless chicken breasts (5 or 6 breasts)

½ teaspoon dried rosemary

½ teaspoon dried thyme

1 teaspoon fine sea salt

½ teaspoon freshly ground black pepper

2 bay leaves

1 (16-ounce) package dried spaghetti pasta, broken in half

1. Select Sauté and add the olive oil to the inner pot. Once the oil is hot, add the onion, garlic, carrots, and celery, and cook for about 3 minutes, until the vegetables start to soften.

2. Press Cancel and pour in the broth. Using a wooden spoon, scrape up any browned bits stuck to the bottom of the pot. Add the chicken, rosemary, thyme, salt, pepper, and bay leaves. Stir to combine.

3. Lock the lid into place. Select Pressure Cook or Manual; set the pressure to High and the time to 10 minutes. Make sure the steam release knob is in the sealed position. After cooking, naturally release the pressure for 10 minutes, then quick release any remaining pressure.

4. Unlock and remove the lid. Remove and discard the bay leaves. Using tongs or a slotted spoon, transfer the chicken to a cutting board. Use two forks to shred the chicken.

5. Select Sauté. Bring the soup to a simmer, then stir in the pasta. Let the pasta cook, uncovered, for about 11 minutes or according to the package instructions. Press Cancel and stir in the shredded chicken.

6. Serve immediately, or place the soup in an airtight container and refrigerate for up to 4 days.

COOKING TIP: *You can use whatever pasta you like, just adjust the cooking time according to the package directions.*

SAUSAGE, WHITE BEAN, AND KALE SOUP

SERVES 6

PREP AND FINISHING:
10 MINUTES

SAUTÉ:
5 MINUTES

PRESSURE COOK:
10 MINUTES ON HIGH

RELEASE:
NATURAL FOR
10 MINUTES,
THEN QUICK

TOTAL TIME:
45 MINUTES

DAIRY-FREE
FREEZER FRIENDLY
GLUTEN-FREE (SEE TIP)
ONE POT

PER SERVING
Calories: 525; Fat: 29g;
Carbohydrates: 42g;
Fiber: 15g; Protein: 24g;
Sodium: 854mg

Even kale skeptics agree that it goes really well with the spicy sausage in this soup. The kale is tender after it's cooked, and the white beans add a thick and chunky texture. This is one of those dishes that tastes even better the day after it's made, making it an ideal meal prep option.

2 tablespoons extra-virgin olive oil
1 medium yellow onion, diced
3 garlic cloves, minced
4 carrots, peeled and chopped
3 celery stalks, sliced
1 pound spicy sausage, sliced into ¾-inch-thick pieces
6 cups low-sodium chicken broth
1 (5-ounce) bag baby kale
2 (15-ounce) cans white beans, drained and rinsed
Juice of 1 lemon

1. Select Sauté and add the olive oil. Once the oil is hot, add the onion, garlic, carrots, celery, and sausage, and cook for 3 minutes.

2. Press Cancel and pour in the broth. Using a wooden spoon, scrape up any browned bits stuck to the bottom of the pot. Add the kale and beans and stir to combine.

3. Lock the lid into place. Select Pressure Cook or Manual; set the pressure to High and the time to 10 minutes. Make sure the steam release knob is in the sealed position. After cooking, naturally release the pressure for 10 minutes, then quick release any remaining pressure.

4. Unlock and remove the lid. Using an immersion blender, blend the soup about halfway so the beans and vegetables are still chunky. Stir in the lemon juice.

5. Serve immediately, or place the soup in an airtight container and refrigerate for up to 4 days or freeze up to 2 months.

INGREDIENT VARIATION: *You can use baby spinach instead of kale, if you prefer.*

GLUTEN-FREE OPTION: *Make sure the sausage is gluten-free. Some is made using gluten products.*

SPLIT PEA SOUP

SERVES 6

PREP AND FINISHING:
10 MINUTES

SAUTÉ:
5 MINUTES

PRESSURE COOK:
15 MINUTES ON HIGH

RELEASE:
NATURAL FOR
10 MINUTES,
THEN QUICK

TOTAL TIME:
50 MINUTES

DAIRY-FREE
FREEZER FRIENDLY
GLUTEN-FREE (SEE TIP)
ONE POT
VEGAN (SEE TIP)

PER SERVING
Calories: 388; Fat: 8g;
Carbohydrates: 55g;
Fiber: 21g; Protein: 26g;
Sodium: 676mg

If I could pick only one soup to make on a cold, wintery day, it would be this one. The smoky ham flavor combined with the tender split peas creates just about the most comforting meal I could ever want. Less than an hour to make from start to finish, it appears on my weekly meal plan often.

2 tablespoons extra-virgin olive oil

1 medium yellow onion, chopped

3 garlic cloves, minced

4 carrots, peeled and sliced

2 celery stalks, sliced

6 cups low-sodium chicken broth

1 (6-ounce) ham steak, cubed

1 pound green split peas, rinsed and drained

1 teaspoon dried oregano

½ teaspoon dried thyme

1 teaspoon fine sea salt

½ teaspoon freshly ground black pepper

1. Select Sauté and add the olive oil to the inner pot. Once the oil is hot, add the onion, garlic, carrots, and celery, and cook for 3 minutes, until the vegetables start to soften.

2. Press Cancel and pour in the broth. Using a wooden spoon, scrape up any browned bits stuck to the bottom of the pot. Add the ham, split peas, oregano, and thyme, and stir to combine.

3. Lock the lid into place. Select Pressure Cook or Manual; set the pressure to High and the time to 15 minutes. Make sure the steam release knob is in the sealed position. After cooking, naturally release the pressure for 10 minutes, then quick release any remaining pressure.

4. Unlock and remove the lid. Stir in the salt and pepper.

5. Serve immediately, or place the soup in an airtight container and refrigerate for up to 4 days or freeze for up to 2 months.

VEGAN OPTION: *Use vegetable broth and leave out the ham to make this dish vegan.*

GLUTEN-FREE OPTION: *Make sure the ham is gluten-free. Some is processed with gluten products.*

BEEF GOULASH

SERVES 6

PREP AND FINISHING:
10 MINUTES

SAUTÉ:
5 MINUTES

PRESSURE COOK:
10 MINUTES ON HIGH

RELEASE:
NATURAL FOR
5 MINUTES,
THEN QUICK

TOTAL TIME:
40 MINUTES

DAIRY-FREE
FREEZER FRIENDLY
GLUTEN-FREE
ONE POT

PER SERVING
Calories: 400; Fat: 20g;
Carbohydrates: 9g;
Fiber: 3g; Protein: 43g;
Sodium: 723mg

Goulash is a stew made with meat and spices that originally comes from Eastern Europe. The American version is made with ground beef, pasta, and a variety of seasonings, and it's an easy, budget-friendly dish perfect for meal prepping. Hot paprika is the traditional spice used in goulash, but I like to use regular paprika instead, since it's much more readily available.

1 tablespoon extra-virgin olive oil

2 pounds 90% lean ground beef

1 medium yellow onion, chopped

3 garlic cloves, minced

2 cups low-sodium beef broth

1 (14.5-ounce) can tomato sauce

1 (14.5-ounce) can diced tomatoes

1 teaspoon dried thyme

2 teaspoons paprika

2 bay leaves

Juice of ½ medium lemon

1 teaspoon fine sea salt

½ teaspoon freshly ground black pepper

1 tablespoon balsamic vinegar

1. Select Sauté and add the olive oil to the inner pot. Once the oil is hot, add the beef, onion, and garlic and sauté for about 3 minutes, stirring occasionally to break up the meat.

2. Press Cancel and pour in the broth. Using a wooden spoon, scrape any browned bits stuck to the bottom of the pot. Stir in the tomato sauce, diced tomatoes, thyme, paprika, and bay leaves.

3. Lock the lid into place. Select Pressure Cook or Manual; set the pressure to High and the time to 10 minutes. Make sure the steam release knob is in the sealed position. After cooking, naturally release the pressure for 5 minutes, then quick release any remaining pressure.

4. Unlock and remove the lid. Stir in the lemon juice, salt, pepper, and vinegar. Using tongs, remove and discard the bay leaves.

5. Serve immediately, or place the goulash in an airtight container and refrigerate for up to 4 days or freeze for up to 2 months.

INGREDIENT VARIATION:
You can use chili powder if you don't have paprika.

CLASSIC BEEF STEW

SERVES 6

PREP AND FINISHING:
10 MINUTES

SAUTÉ:
5 MINUTES

PRESSURE COOK:
30 MINUTES ON HIGH

RELEASE:
NATURAL FOR
10 MINUTES,
THEN QUICK

TOTAL TIME:
1 HOUR, 5 MINUTES

DAIRY-FREE
FREEZER FRIENDLY
GLUTEN-FREE (SEE TIP)
ONE POT

PER SERVING
Calories: 378; Fat: 14g;
Carbohydrates: 25g;
Fiber: 5g; Protein: 37g;
Sodium: 415mg

There is just something so cozy and nourishing about a beef stew full of hearty vegetables and potatoes. This is one of my husband's favorite recipes of all time. I love that I can make it in less than half the time it used to take on the stovetop. The beef literally falls apart in your mouth, and the veggies and potatoes are tender and full of flavor.

2 tablespoons extra-virgin olive oil
2 pounds beef stew meat, cut into 1-inch cubes
3 cups low-sodium beef broth
1 pound red potatoes, cut into 1-inch chunks
1 medium yellow onion, diced
3 garlic cloves, minced
4 carrots, peeled and chopped
4 celery stalks, chopped
¼ cup tomato paste
1 teaspoon fine sea salt
½ teaspoon freshly ground black pepper
1 teaspoon dried thyme
1 teaspoon dried oregano
1 cup frozen peas

1. Select Sauté and add the olive oil. Once the oil is hot, add the beef and sauté for 3 minutes, using a spatula to move the pieces around so they start to brown on all sides.

2. Press Cancel and pour in the broth. Using a wooden spoon, scrape up any browned bits stuck to the bottom of the pot. Add the potatoes, onion, garlic, carrots, celery, tomato paste, salt, pepper, thyme, and oregano, and stir to combine.

3. Lock the lid into place. Select Pressure Cook or Manual; set the pressure to High and the time to 30 minutes. Make sure the steam release knob is in the sealed position. After cooking, naturally release the pressure for 10 minutes, then quick release any remaining pressure.

4. Unlock and remove the lid. Stir in the frozen peas. Let the peas warm through, about 5 minutes.

5. Serve immediately, or place the stew in an airtight container and refrigerate for up to 4 days or freeze up to 2 months.

INGREDIENT VARIATION: *For a lower-carb version of this dish, swap out the potatoes for 2 large zucchini, sliced into ½-inch-thick pieces (about 4 cups).*

GLUTEN-FREE OPTION: *Make sure the tomato paste is gluten-free. Some brands are processed with gluten products.*

SWEET POTATO AND GROUND TURKEY CHILI

SERVES 8

PREP AND FINISHING:
10 MINUTES

SAUTÉ:
5 MINUTES

PRESSURE COOK:
10 MINUTES ON HIGH

RELEASE:
NATURAL FOR
10 MINUTES,
THEN QUICK

TOTAL TIME:
45 MINUTES

**ADVANCE PREP
(SEE TIP)**
DAIRY-FREE
FREEZER FRIENDLY
GLUTEN-FREE
ONE POT

PER SERVING
Calories: 230; Fat: 6g;
Carbohydrates: 16g;
Fiber: 3g; Protein: 29g;
Sodium: 138mg

This bean-free chili has tons of flavor and heartiness from the ground turkey, vegetables, and sweet potato. The spices aren't too strong, so it's kid friendly as well. As delicious as this chili is, the leftovers almost seem to taste better than the first serving. It is perfect for potlucks, weeknight meals, or anytime you want something easy, hearty, and delicious.

2 tablespoons extra-virgin olive oil

2 pounds ground turkey

3 medium sweet potatoes, peeled and cut into 1-inch cubes

1 medium red or white onion, diced

3 garlic cloves, minced

4 celery stalks, chopped

3 carrots, peeled and chopped

1 red bell pepper, seeded and chopped

1 (14.5-ounce) can diced tomatoes

3 cups low-sodium chicken broth

½ teaspoon ground cumin

½ teaspoon chili powder

¼ teaspoon fine sea salt (optional)

Fresh, chopped cilantro, for garnish (optional)

1. Select Sauté and add the olive oil to the inner pot. Once the oil is hot, add the ground turkey. Cook for 2 minutes, using a wooden spoon to break up the meat and keep it from sticking to the pot.

2. Press Cancel and add the sweet potatoes, onion, garlic, celery, carrots, bell pepper, tomatoes, and chicken broth to the pot.

3. Lock the lid into place. Select Pressure Cook or Manual; set the pressure to High and the time to 10 minutes. Make sure the steam release knob is in the sealed position. After cooking, naturally release the pressure for 10 minutes, then quick release any remaining pressure.

4. Unlock and remove the lid. Stir in the cumin, chili powder, and salt (if using).

5. Serve immediately garnished with fresh cilantro, or place the chili in an airtight container and refrigerate for up to 4 days or freeze for up to 2 months.

ADVANCE PREP TIP: *Chop all of the vegetables and store them in an airtight container in the refrigerator for up to 1 week before cooking.*

MEAL PREP TIP: *You can serve this chili with cooked brown rice (page 22) or basmati rice (page 20). It also goes really well with a few slices of fresh avocado per serving.*

HEARTY BEEF CHILI

SERVES 8

PREP AND FINISHING:
10 MINUTES

SAUTÉ:
5 MINUTES

PRESSURE COOK:
10 MINUTES ON HIGH

RELEASE:
NATURAL FOR
10 MINUTES,
THEN QUICK

TOTAL TIME:
45 MINUTES

DAIRY-FREE
FREEZER FRIENDLY
GLUTEN-FREE (SEE TIP)
ONE POT

PER SERVING
Calories: 340; Fat: 14g;
Carbohydrates: 20g;
Fiber: 7g; Protein: 31g;
Sodium: 621mg

Stovetop chili, begone. Just add everything to the Instant Pot®, walk away, and let it do all the work. It's a favorite for potlucks, game days, or anytime you want to serve a crowd. This version is not too spicy, with a rich tomato flavor and a tiny bit of sweetness from the Worcestershire sauce.

2 tablespoons extra-virgin olive oil

1 medium yellow onion, diced

3 garlic cloves, minced

2 pounds 90% lean ground beef

1 teaspoon chili powder

½ teaspoon ground cumin

4 cups low-sodium beef broth

1 (28-ounce) can crushed tomatoes

1 (14.5-ounce) can kidney beans, drained and rinsed

1 teaspoon Worcestershire sauce

1. Select Sauté and add the olive oil to the inner pot. Once the oil is hot, add the onion, garlic, ground beef, chili powder, and cumin and cook for 3 minutes, until the beef starts to brown.

2. Press Cancel and pour in the broth. Using a wooden spoon, scrape up any browned bits stuck to the bottom of the pot. Add the tomatoes and beans, but don't stir.

3. Lock the lid into place. Select Pressure Cook or Manual; set the pressure to High and the time to 10 minutes. Make sure the steam release knob is in the sealed position. After cooking, naturally release the pressure for 10 minutes, then quick release any remaining pressure.

4. Unlock and remove the lid. Stir in the Worcestershire sauce.

5. Serve immediately, or place the chili in an airtight container and refrigerate for up to 4 days or freeze for up to 2 months.

INGREDIENT VARIATION: *Instead of kidney beans, you can use canned white beans, black beans, or navy beans.*

GLUTEN-FREE OPTION: *Make sure you use Worcestershire sauce that is labeled gluten-free.*

Shredded Chicken and Rice Burrito Bowl, page 132

6

Seafood and Poultry Mains

LEMON-GARLIC SHRIMP SCAMPI

SERVES 8

PREP AND FINISHING:
10 MINUTES

SAUTÉ:
5 MINUTES

PRESSURE COOK:
2 MINUTES ON HIGH

RELEASE:
NATURAL FOR
5 MINUTES,
THEN QUICK

TOTAL TIME:
32 MINUTES

**ADVANCE PREP
(SEE TIP)**
GLUTEN-FREE (SEE TIP)

PER SERVING
Calories: 252; Fat: 8g;
Carbohydrates: 16g;
Fiber: 3g; Protein: 27g;
Sodium: 398mg

Shrimp scampi is one of those recipes that's fancy enough for a dinner party and also easy enough for a quick weeknight dinner. I recommend serving the shrimp with whole-wheat spaghetti to soak up all the vibrant sauce. This dish makes excellent leftovers.

2 tablespoons extra-virgin olive oil

2 tablespoons unsalted butter

2 garlic cloves, minced

½ cup white wine

½ cup low-sodium chicken broth

2 pounds fresh or frozen shrimp, peeled and deveined

1 (16-ounce) package dried whole-wheat spaghetti pasta, cooked according to package directions

Juice of 1 lemon

½ teaspoon fine sea salt

¼ teaspoon freshly ground black pepper

1. Select Sauté and add the olive oil and butter to the inner pot. Once the oil is hot and the butter has melted, add the garlic and sauté for 2 minutes.

2. Press Cancel and add the wine and chicken broth. Using a wooden spoon, scrape up any browned bits stuck to the bottom of the pot. Add the shrimp to the pot. Stir to combine.

3. Lock the lid into place. Select Pressure Cook or Manual; set the pressure to High and the time to 2 minutes (4 minutes if using frozen shrimp). Make sure the steam release knob is in the sealed position. After cooking, naturally release the pressure for 5 minutes, then quick release any remaining pressure.

4. Unlock and remove the lid. Stir in the pasta, lemon juice, salt, and pepper.

5. Serve immediately, or place the shrimp and pasta in an airtight container and refrigerate for up to 4 days.

ADVANCE PREP TIP: *Cook and drain the spaghetti up to 3 days ahead of time. Store it in an airtight container in the refrigerator until you're ready to make this dish.*

GLUTEN-FREE OPTION: *Use brown rice spaghetti in place of the whole-wheat version.*

SPICY SHRIMP AND GRITS

SERVES 6

PREP AND FINISHING:
15 MINUTES

SAUTÉ:
10 MINUTES

PRESSURE COOK:
10 MINUTES ON HIGH

RELEASE:
NATURAL FOR
10 MINUTES,
THEN QUICK

TOTAL TIME:
55 MINUTES

GLUTEN-FREE
ONE POT

PER SERVING
Calories: 394; Fat: 9g;
Carbohydrates: 63g;
Fiber: 5g; Protein: 18g;
Sodium: 339mg

Grits are made from corn and are mild and creamy after they've been cooked. Making grits on the stovetop can be time consuming and messy, because they tend to boil over. But the Instant Pot® cooks them perfectly and without any mess. The spicy shrimp is delicious served on top of the creamy grits. Shrimp and grits is a classic combo for a reason!

2 tablespoons extra-virgin olive oil

1 pound medium shrimp, peeled and deveined, tails left on

2 garlic cloves, minced

½ teaspoon chili powder

1 cup low-sodium chicken broth

1 tablespoon unsalted butter

½ teaspoon fine sea salt

2 cups cornmeal grits

4 cups water

1. Select Sauté and add the olive oil to the inner pot. Once the oil is hot, add the shrimp, garlic, and chili powder and sauté for about 5 minutes, stirring occasionally so the shrimp are cooked through on both sides.

2. Press Cancel. Using a slotted spoon, transfer the shrimp and garlic to a serving plate. Cover to keep warm.

3. Pour the broth into the pot. Using a wooden spoon, scrape up any browned bits stuck to the bottom of the pot. Add the butter, salt, grits, and water to the pot.

4. Lock the lid into place. Select Pressure Cook or Manual; set the pressure to High and the time to 10 minutes. Make sure the steam release knob is in the sealed position. After cooking, naturally release the pressure for 10 minutes, then quick release any remaining pressure.

5. Unlock and remove the lid. Stir the grits.

6. To serve immediately, divide the grits among individual serving plates and top with the shrimp. To store for later, transfer the grits to individual airtight containers, top each portion with some shrimp, and refrigerate for up to 4 days.

COOKING TIP: *You can use fresh or frozen shrimp for this recipe. If you use frozen shrimp, let them defrost overnight in the fridge before cooking.*

MEAL PREP TIP: *It's traditional to add cheese to grits, so a nice option for this dish is to top each serving with 1 tablespoon of grated Parmesan or cheddar cheese.*

SALMON AND VEGETABLES WITH LEMON-BUTTER SAUCE

SERVES 5

PREP AND FINISHING:
10 MINUTES

PRESSURE COOK:
5 MINUTES ON HIGH

RELEASE:
NATURAL FOR
10 MINUTES,
THEN QUICK

TOTAL TIME:
35 MINUTES

**GLUTEN-FREE
ONE POT**

PER SERVING
Calories: 362; Fat: 14g;
Carbohydrates: 34g;
Fiber: 4g; Protein: 27g;
Sodium: 563mg

Don't you love when a show-stopping dish is actually one of the simplest to make? This recipe is the perfect example. You don't even have to plan ahead, just grab salmon fillets out of the freezer and cook them right along with red potatoes and carrots. The butter sauce coats everything and makes for a flavorful, healthy meal.

1 cup low-sodium vegetable broth

2 pounds medium red potatoes, cut into 1-inch chunks

4 carrots, peeled and chopped into 1-inch-thick pieces (about 2 cups)

5 (4-ounce) frozen salmon fillets

4 tablespoons unsalted butter, melted

1 teaspoon fine sea salt

½ teaspoon garlic powder

Juice of 2 lemons

Freshly ground black pepper

Fresh chopped dill, for garnish (optional)

1. Pour the broth into the inner pot and add the potatoes and carrots. Place the salmon fillets, skin-side down, on top of the vegetables.

2. Pour the melted butter over the salmon and sprinkle the salt and garlic powder over the top.

SALMON AND VEGETABLES WITH LEMON-BUTTER SAUCE *continues*

3. Lock the lid into place. Select Pressure Cook or Manual; set the pressure to High and the time to 5 minutes. Make sure the steam release knob is in the sealed position. After cooking, naturally release the pressure for 10 minutes, then quick release any remaining pressure.

4. Unlock and remove the lid. Serve immediately garnished with black pepper and dill, or place the salmon and vegetables in an airtight container and refrigerate for up to 4 days.

COOKING TIP: *If your salmon fillets are larger than 4 ounces, you might be able to fit only four in the pot at one time. Also, be sure to cut your potatoes and vegetables fairly small so they cook all the way through during the short cooking time.*

SEAFOOD GUMBO

SERVES 6

PREP AND FINISHING:
10 MINUTES

SAUTÉ:
5 MINUTES

PRESSURE COOK:
5 MINUTES ON HIGH

RELEASE:
NATURAL FOR
5 MINUTES,
THEN QUICK

TOTAL TIME:
35 MINUTES

DAIRY-FREE
GLUTEN-FREE
ONE POT

PER SERVING
Calories: 209; Fat: 7g;
Carbohydrates: 6g;
Fiber: 2g; Protein: 28g;
Sodium: 383mg

A gumbo is a tomato-based stew made with different types of seafood. I've simplified this recipe, using white fish and shrimp and a homemade blend of spices to give it a real Cajun feel. In just over half an hour, you'll be rewarded with a thick, hearty, and spicy meal that you can serve on its own or over white rice.

2 tablespoons extra-virgin olive oil

1 medium yellow onion, diced

2 garlic cloves, minced

2 celery stalks, diced

2 cups low-sodium chicken broth

1 (14-ounce) can diced tomatoes

1 pound halibut fillets, patted dry and cut into
2-inch cubes

1 pound medium shrimp, peeled and deveined,
tails left on

½ teaspoon cayenne pepper

1 teaspoon dried oregano

1 teaspoon dried thyme

2 teaspoon paprika

½ teaspoon fine sea salt

½ teaspoon freshly ground black pepper

SEAFOOD GUMBO *continues*

1. Select Sauté and add the olive oil to the inner pot. Once the oil is hot, add the onion, garlic, and celery and sauté for 3 minutes, stirring occasionally.

2. Press Cancel and pour the broth and diced tomatoes into the pot. Using a wooden spoon, scrape up any browned bits stuck to the bottom of the pot. Add the halibut, shrimp, cayenne pepper, oregano, thyme, paprika, salt, and pepper. Stir to combine.

3. Lock the lid into place. Select Pressure Cook or Manual; set the pressure to High and the time to 5 minutes. Make sure the steam release knob is in the sealed position. After cooking, naturally release the pressure for 5 minutes, then quick release any remaining pressure.

4. Unlock and remove the lid. Stir the gumbo.

5. Serve immediately, or place the gumbo in an airtight container and refrigerate for up to 4 days.

INGREDIENT VARIATION: *You can use whatever firm fish you like in this recipe, including sea bass, salmon, or cod.*

COCONUT FISH CURRY

SERVES 6

PREP AND FINISHING:
10 MINUTES

SAUTÉ:
5 MINUTES

PRESSURE COOK:
4 MINUTES ON HIGH

RELEASE:
NATURAL FOR
10 MINUTES,
THEN QUICK

TOTAL TIME:
39 MINUTES

DAIRY-FREE
FREEZER FRIENDLY
GLUTEN-FREE (SEE TIP)
ONE POT

PER SERVING
Calories: 362; Fat: 25g;
Carbohydrates: 12g;
Fiber: 3g; Protein: 24g;
Sodium: 459mg

This recipe is inspired by a fish curry I had while on vacation on the island of Maui in Hawaii. I make my version with firm white fish and canned coconut milk, and the fish comes out perfectly cooked, surrounded by flavorful broth and lots of crunchy vegetables. I like to serve this dish Hawaiian-style in a shallow bowl with a scoop of basmati rice (page 20) on the side.

2 tablespoons extra-virgin olive oil

1 white onion, sliced

1½ pounds mahi mahi fillets (about 4 fillets), cut into 2-inch cubes

1 tablespoon green curry paste

1 (13.5-ounce) can full-fat coconut milk

2 tablespoons reduced-sodium soy sauce

1 tablespoon brown sugar

½ teaspoon ground ginger

2 red bell peppers, seeded and sliced

Juice of 1 lime

1. Select Sauté and add the olive oil to the inner pot. Once the oil is hot, add the onion, fish, and green curry paste; sauté for about 4 minutes, stirring occasionally, until the fish is browned on all sides.

2. Press Cancel and add the coconut milk, soy sauce, brown sugar, and ginger. Using a wooden spoon, scrape up any browned bits stuck to the bottom of the pot. Add the bell peppers and stir to combine.

COCONUT FISH CURRY *continues*

3. Lock the lid into place. Select Pressure Cook or Manual; set the pressure to High and the time to 4 minutes. Make sure the steam release knob is in the sealed position. After cooking, naturally release the pressure for 10 minutes, then quick release any remaining pressure.

4. Unlock and remove the lid. Stir in the lime juice.

5. Serve immediately, or place the curry in an airtight container and refrigerate for up to 4 days or freeze up to 2 months.

MEAL PREP TIP: *If you can't find mahi mahi, you can also use halibut in this recipe. This dish is great served with cooked white or brown rice.*

GLUTEN-FREE OPTION: *Use tamari in place of the soy sauce.*

CHICKEN CACCIATORE

SERVES 6

PREP AND FINISHING:
10 MINUTES

SAUTÉ:
10 MINUTES

PRESSURE COOK:
12 MINUTES ON HIGH

RELEASE:
NATURAL FOR
10 MINUTES,
THEN QUICK

TOTAL TIME:
52 MINUTES

DAIRY-FREE
FREEZER FRIENDLY
GLUTEN-FREE
ONE POT

PER SERVING
Calories: 269; Fat: 7g;
Carbohydrates: 12g;
Fiber: 3g; Protein: 38g;
Sodium: 393mg

Traditional chicken cacciatore is a classic Italian dish that is cooked on the stovetop or in the oven. As with most other recipes, the Instant Pot® makes it so much faster, without any loss of authentic quality. It's full of rich tomato flavor from both the crushed tomatoes and the tomato paste. Serve it over pasta, mashed potatoes, or polenta for an easy and satisfying lunch or dinner.

2 tablespoons extra-virgin olive oil

2 pounds boneless, skinless chicken breasts (5 or 6 breasts)

2 garlic cloves, minced

1 medium yellow onion, diced

½ teaspoon dried oregano

½ teaspoon fine sea salt

½ cup white wine

½ cup low-sodium chicken broth

2 red bell peppers, seeded and sliced

1 cup button mushrooms, sliced

1 (14-ounce) can crushed tomatoes

½ teaspoon freshly ground black pepper

1 tablespoon balsamic vinegar

1. Select Sauté and add the olive oil to the inner pot. Once the oil is hot, add the chicken, garlic, onion, oregano, and salt and sauté for 3 minutes, stirring occasionally. Turn the chicken once and sauté for 3 minutes more, so both sides start to brown.

CHICKEN CACCIATORE *continues*

2. Press Cancel and pour the wine into the pot. Using a wooden spoon, scrape up any browned bits stuck to the bottom of the pot. Add the broth, bell peppers, mushrooms, and crushed tomatoes and stir to combine.

3. Lock the lid into place. Select Pressure Cook or Manual; set the pressure to High and the time to 12 minutes. Make sure the steam release knob is in the sealed position. After cooking, naturally release the pressure for 10 minutes, then quick release any remaining pressure.

4. Unlock and remove the lid. Stir in the black pepper and vinegar.

5. Serve immediately, or place the cacciatore in an airtight container and refrigerate for up to 4 days or freeze for up to 2 months.

INGREDIENT VARIATION: *If you don't have white wine, you can leave it out and increase the chicken broth to 1 cup in total.*

BALSAMIC CHICKEN WITH VEGETABLES AND POTATOES

SERVES 6

PREP AND FINISHING:
10 MINUTES

SAUTÉ:
10 MINUTES

PRESSURE COOK:
10 MINUTES ON HIGH

RELEASE:
NATURAL FOR
10 MINUTES,
THEN QUICK

TOTAL TIME:
50 MINUTES

FREEZER FRIENDLY
GLUTEN-FREE

PER SERVING
Calories: 269; Fat: 9g;
Carbohydrates: 12g;
Fiber: 2g; Protein: 36g;
Sodium: 348mg

This dish is a meal prepper's dream—it cooks all in one pot, it's delicious, and it's packed with nutrients. The chicken is tender with a flavorful, tangy balsamic sauce, and the veggies and potatoes cook at the same time as the chicken, so it's great for easy, fast cleanup.

1 tablespoon cornstarch

½ cup water

2 tablespoons extra-virgin olive oil

2 pounds boneless, skinless chicken breasts (5 or 6 breasts)

2 garlic cloves, minced

1 teaspoon dried thyme

½ teaspoon salt

1 cup low-sodium chicken broth

2 tablespoons balsamic vinegar

½ pound rainbow carrots, peeled and cut into 1-inch-thick pieces

1/2 pound zucchini, cut into 1-inch-thick pieces

½ pound small potatoes, halved

1 tablespoon unsalted butter

1. In a small bowl, make a slurry by whisking together the cornstarch and water. Set aside.

BALSAMIC CHICKEN WITH
VEGETABLES AND POTATOES *continues*

2. Select Sauté and add the olive oil to the inner pot. Once the oil is hot, place the chicken in the pot, along with the garlic, thyme, and salt. Sauté the garlic and chicken for 4 minutes, turning the chicken once so it browns on both sides. Using a spoon, transfer the chicken and garlic to a plate.

3. Press Cancel and add the broth and vinegar. Using a wooden spoon, scrape up any browned bits stuck to the bottom of the pot. Add the carrots, zucchini, and potatoes to the pot. Stir to combine. Place the chicken and garlic on top of the vegetables, but don't stir.

4. Lock the lid into place. Select Pressure Cook or Manual; set the pressure to High and the time to 10 minutes. Make sure the steam release knob is in the sealed position. After cooking, naturally release the pressure for 10 minutes, then quick release any remaining pressure.

5. Unlock and remove the lid. Use a slotted spoon to remove the chicken and vegetables to a serving bowl.

6. Select Sauté. Once the liquid starts bubbling, whisk in the cornstarch slurry and butter until well combined. Whisk consistently for 2 minutes or until the sauce starts to thicken.

7. Press Cancel and return the chicken and vegetables to the pot. Stir to combine. Serve immediately, or place the chicken and vegetables in an airtight container and refrigerate for up to 4 days or freeze for up to 2 months.

MEAL PREP TIP: *You can substitute sliced zucchini for the carrots, if you prefer. Or choose orange, yellow, and purple carrots for a colorful display.*

LEMON PICCATA CHICKEN

SERVES 6

PREP AND FINISHING:
10 MINUTES

SAUTÉ:
10 MINUTES

PRESSURE COOK:
10 MINUTES ON HIGH

RELEASE:
NATURAL FOR
10 MINUTES,
THEN QUICK

TOTAL TIME:
50 MINUTES

**ADVANCE PREP
(SEE TIP)**
FREEZER FRIENDLY
GLUTEN-FREE

PER SERVING
Calories: 250; Fat: 11g;
Carbohydrates: 3g;
Fiber: 0g; Protein: 35g;
Sodium: 371mg

Don't be intimidated by the name of this dish. *Piccata* simply means chicken cooked with tangy capers and served with a bright and creamy lemon-butter sauce. It's as good as it sounds, and this dish is one of my favorite weeknight go-tos. I love to serve it with cooked brown rice (page 22) or basmati rice (page 20) and steamed vegetables (page 18).

2 tablespoons cornstarch

½ cup water

2 tablespoons extra-virgin olive oil

2 pounds boneless, skinless chicken breasts (5 or 6 breasts)

1½ cups low-sodium chicken broth

⅓ cup capers, drained and rinsed

2 tablespoons unsalted butter

Juice of 2 medium lemons

¼ teaspoon fine sea salt (optional)

1. In a small bowl, make a slurry by whisking together the cornstarch and water. Set aside.

2. Select Sauté and add the olive oil to the inner pot. Once the oil is hot, place the chicken breasts in the pot and brown them for 2 minutes per side.

3. Press Cancel and add the broth and capers. Using a wooden spoon, scrape up any browned bits stuck to the bottom of the pot.

4. Lock the lid into place. Select Pressure Cook or Manual; set the pressure to High and the time to 10 minutes. Make sure the steam release knob is in the sealed position. After cooking, naturally release the pressure for 10 minutes, then quick release any remaining pressure.

5. Unlock and remove the lid. Use a slotted spoon to remove the chicken to a plate.

6. Select Sauté. Once the liquid starts bubbling, whisk in the cornstarch slurry and butter. Whisk constantly for 2 minutes or until the sauce starts to thicken.

7. Press Cancel and return the chicken to the pot with the sauce, along with the lemon juice and salt (if using).

8. Serve immediately, or place the chicken and sauce in an airtight container and refrigerate for up to 4 days or freeze for up to 2 months.

ADVANCE PREP TIP: *Juice the lemons up to 3 days ahead of time and store in a tightly covered jar in the refrigerator. You can also rinse and drain the capers in advance of making this dish; store them in the refrigerator for up to a week.*

MEAL PREP TIP: *It's nice to serve the leftovers of this dish with fresh lemon wedges to enhance the lemon flavor.*

EASY CHICKEN FAJITAS

SERVES 6

PREP AND FINISHING:
10 MINUTES

SAUTÉ:
5 MINUTES

PRESSURE COOK:
10 MINUTES ON HIGH

RELEASE:
NATURAL FOR
10 MINUTES,
THEN QUICK

TOTAL TIME:
45 MINUTES

**DAIRY-FREE
FREEZER FRIENDLY
GLUTEN-FREE
ONE POT**

PER SERVING
Calories: 237; Fat: 7g;
Carbohydrates: 9g;
Fiber: 2g; Protein: 36g;
Sodium: 420mg

These fajitas have all the authentic Mexican flavors without the fuss of grilling. Serve them straight out of the pot or spoon them over Spanish Rice (page 51) or into tortillas or taco shells.

2 tablespoons extra-virgin olive oil

2 pounds boneless, skinless chicken breasts (5 or 6 breasts), cut into 1-inch-thick strips

2 red bell peppers, seeded and sliced

2 yellow bell peppers, seeded and sliced

2 garlic cloves, minced

1 medium yellow onion, diced

1 teaspoon ground cumin

1 teaspoon chili powder

1 teaspoon fine sea salt

½ teaspoon freshly ground black pepper

½ cup water

Juice of 2 limes

1. Select Sauté and add the olive oil to the inner pot. Once the oil is hot, add the chicken strips, bell peppers, garlic, onion, cumin, chili powder, salt, and black pepper; sauté for 2 minutes.

2. Press Cancel and pour in the water. Using a wooden spoon, scrape up any browned bits stuck to the bottom of the pot.

3. Lock the lid into place. Select Pressure Cook or Manual; set the pressure to High and the time to 10 minutes. Make sure the steam release knob is in the sealed position. After cooking, naturally release the pressure for 10 minutes, then quick release any remaining pressure.

4. Unlock and remove the lid. Stir in the lime juice.

5. Serve immediately, or place the chicken and vegetables in an airtight container and refrigerate for up to 4 days or freeze for up to 2 months.

COOKING TIP: *Feel free to layer on the toppings to give the fajitas even more flavor, including sliced avocado or prepared guacamole, jarred or fresh salsa, and/or shredded Cheddar cheese.*

TERIYAKI CHICKEN AND RICE

SERVES 6

PREP AND FINISHING:
10 MINUTES

SAUTÉ:
5 MINUTES

PRESSURE COOK:
8 MINUTES ON HIGH

RELEASE:
NATURAL FOR
10 MINUTES,
THEN QUICK

TOTAL TIME:
43 MINUTES

DAIRY-FREE
FREEZER FRIENDLY
GLUTEN-FREE (SEE TIP)
ONE POT

PER SERVING
Calories: 371; Fat: 7g;
Carbohydrates: 45g;
Fiber: 1g; Protein: 31g;
Sodium: 484mg

This is one of the easiest recipes I've ever made in the Instant Pot® but also one of my favorites. Kids love it because it's slightly sweet from the homemade teriyaki sauce, but it's also great as a basic one-pot lunch or dinner for everyone. The rice is cooked perfectly, and the chicken is moist and tender with the perfect balance of sweet and sour.

2 tablespoons extra-virgin olive oil

2 garlic cloves, minced

1½ pounds boneless, skinless chicken breasts (4 or 5 breasts)

¼ cup reduced-sodium soy sauce

1¾ cups low-sodium chicken broth

2 tablespoons pure maple syrup

½ teaspoon ground ginger

2 carrots, peeled and sliced (about 1 cup)

1½ cups white rice, rinsed (see Cooking Tip)

1 tablespoon white wine vinegar

1. Select Sauté and add the olive oil to the inner pot. Once the oil is hot, add the garlic and chicken and sauté for 4 minutes, turning the chicken once so it browns on both sides. Use a spoon to transfer the chicken and garlic to a plate.

2. Press Cancel and add the soy sauce. Using a wooden spoon, scrape up any browned bits stuck to the bottom of the pot. Add the broth, maple syrup, ginger, carrots, and rice to the pot. Stir to combine. Place the chicken on top, but don't stir.

3. Lock the lid into place. Select Pressure Cook or Manual; set the pressure to High and the time to 8 minutes. Make sure the steam release knob is in the sealed position. After cooking, naturally release the pressure for 10 minutes, then quick release any remaining pressure.

4. Unlock and remove the lid. Stir in the vinegar.

5. Serve immediately, or place the chicken and rice in an airtight container and refrigerate for up to 4 days or freeze for up to 2 months.

COOKING TIP: *Use a fine-mesh strainer to rinse the rice just before you add it to the pot. This is a necessary step to add enough moisture to keep the rice from burning.*

GLUTEN-FREE OPTION: *Use tamari sauce in place of the soy sauce.*

SHREDDED CHICKEN AND RICE BURRITO BOWL

SERVES 6

PREP AND FINISHING:
10 MINUTES

SAUTÉ:
5 MINUTES

PRESSURE COOK:
15 MINUTES ON HIGH

RELEASE:
NATURAL FOR
10 MINUTES,
THEN QUICK

TOTAL TIME:
50 MINUTES

**ADVANCE PREP
(SEE TIP)
DAIRY-FREE
FREEZER FRIENDLY
GLUTEN-FREE**

PER SERVING
Calories: 423; Fat: 12g;
Carbohydrates: 37g;
Fiber: 8g; Protein: 43g;
Sodium: 332mg

If you're a fan of those giant chicken burritos wrapped in foil that you can get from food trucks or roadside vendors, then you'll love this chicken and rice burrito bowl. For a healthy spin, I swap out the tortilla for brown rice and leave off the cheese in favor of avocado. The rice also helps soak up the flavorful, nourishing broth.

2 tablespoons extra-virgin olive oil

2 pounds boneless, skinless chicken breasts (5 or 6 breasts)

1 teaspoon ground cumin

¼ teaspoon cayenne pepper or taco seasoning

1 medium red or white onion, chopped

1 (4-ounce) can chopped or diced green chiles

1½ cups low-sodium chicken broth

1 (15-ounce) can pinto beans, drained and rinsed

3 cups cooked brown rice (page 22)

2 medium avocados, pitted and sliced, for garnish

Fresh chopped cilantro, for garnish

Sliced jalapeño, for garnish

Prepared salsa, for garnish (optional)

1. Select Sauté and add the olive oil to the inner pot. Once the oil is hot, place the chicken breasts in the pot and brown them for 2 minutes per side.

2. Press Cancel and add the cumin, cayenne pepper, onion, green chiles, and chicken broth. Using a wooden spoon, scrape up any browned bits stuck to the bottom of the pot.

3. Lock the lid into place. Select Pressure Cook or Manual; set the pressure to High and the time to 15 minutes. Make sure the steam release knob is in the sealed position. After cooking, naturally release the pressure for 10 minutes, then quick release any remaining pressure.

4. Unlock and remove the lid. Use a slotted spoon to transfer the chicken to a cutting board. Shred the chicken using two forks, and then add it back to the pot. Add the pinto beans and stir the ingredients to combine.

5. Serve immediately, or place the chicken and rice in an airtight container and refrigerate for up to 4 days or freeze for up to 2 months.

6. When ready to serve, divide the rice among six bowls and ladle the chicken mixture on top. Garnish each bowl with 2 slices of fresh avocado, cilantro, jalapeño, and a spoonful of salsa (if using).

ADVANCE PREP TIP: *Prepare the rice ahead of time and warm it up before serving.*

MEAL PREP TIP: *Slice the avocado right before serving to keep it from browning.*

KUNG PAO CHICKEN

SERVES 6

PREP AND FINISHING:
10 MINUTES

SAUTÉ:
10 MINUTES

PRESSURE COOK:
8 MINUTES ON HIGH

RELEASE:
NATURAL FOR
10 MINUTES,
THEN QUICK

TOTAL TIME:
48 MINUTES

DAIRY-FREE
FREEZER FRIENDLY
GLUTEN-FREE (SEE TIP)

PER SERVING
Calories: 270; Fat: 8g;
Carbohydrates: 13g;
Fiber: 2g; Protein: 38g;
Sodium: 470mg

If you like sweet and spicy flavors together, you'll want to make this takeout favorite as soon as possible. The chicken is fully coated with the sauce; the chopped peanuts add crunch. I like to serve this dish over riced cauliflower or basmati rice (page 20).

2 tablespoons cornstarch

½ cup water

1 tablespoon extra-virgin olive oil

2 garlic cloves, minced

1 onion, diced

2 pounds boneless, skinless chicken breasts (5 or 6 breasts), cut into bite-size pieces

1 cup low-sodium chicken broth

2 red bell peppers, seeded and sliced

¼ cup reduced-sodium soy sauce or tamari

2 tablespoons brown sugar

¼ teaspoon ground ginger

¼ teaspoon red pepper flakes

2 tablespoons rice vinegar

¼ cup chopped roasted peanuts

1. In a small bowl, make a slurry by whisking together the cornstarch and water. Set aside.

2. Select Sauté and add the olive oil to the inner pot. Once hot, add the garlic, onion, and chicken and sauté for 2 minutes, stirring occasionally. Turn the chicken over and let the chicken and vegetables cook for 2 minutes more.

3. Press Cancel and pour the broth into the pot. Using a wooden spoon, scrape up any browned bits stuck to the bottom of the pot. Add the bell peppers, soy sauce, brown sugar, ginger, and red pepper flakes, and stir to combine.

4. Lock the lid into place. Select Pressure Cook or Manual; set the pressure to High and the time to 8 minutes. Make sure the steam release knob is in the sealed position. After cooking, let naturally release the pressure for 10 minutes, then quick release any remaining pressure.

5. Unlock and remove the lid. Using a slotted spoon, transfer the chicken to a plate.

6. Select Sauté. Once the liquid starts bubbling, whisk the cornstarch slurry and vinegar. Whisk consistently for 2 minutes or until the sauce starts to thicken.

7. Serve immediately with the chopped peanuts sprinkled on top, or place the chicken in an airtight container and refrigerate for up to 4 days or freeze for up to 2 months.

INGREDIENT VARIATION: *If you don't have rice vinegar, you can use white wine vinegar or apple cider vinegar instead.*

GLUTEN-FREE OPTION: *Use tamari instead of soy sauce.*

HONEY SESAME CHICKEN

SERVES 6

PREP AND FINISHING:
10 MINUTES

SAUTÉ:
10 MINUTES

PRESSURE COOK:
8 MINUTES ON HIGH

RELEASE:
NATURAL FOR
10 MINUTES,
THEN QUICK

TOTAL TIME:
48 MINUTES

**DAIRY-FREE
GLUTEN-FREE (SEE TIP)**

PER SERVING
Calories: 198; Fat: 4g;
Carbohydrates: 13g;
Fiber: 0g; Protein: 27g;
Sodium: 351mg

Sesame chicken was always one of my favorites when I ordered out at Chinese restaurants. When I moved to clean eating, it was my mission to come up with a healthier version. I couldn't be happier with the results. The sauce has the perfect amount of sweetness. For a filling and delicious dinner, serve the chicken over basmati rice (page 20) or brown rice (page 22) with steamed broccoli on the side.

2 tablespoons cornstarch

½ cup water

1 tablespoon extra-virgin olive oil

2 garlic cloves, minced

1 medium yellow onion, diced

2 pounds boneless, skinless chicken breasts (5 or 6 breasts), cut into bite-size pieces

1 cup low-sodium chicken broth

¼ cup reduced-sodium soy sauce

¼ cup honey

2 teaspoons toasted sesame oil

1. In a small bowl, make a slurry by whisking together the cornstarch and water. Set aside.

2. Select Sauté and add the olive oil to the inner pot. Once the oil is hot, add the garlic, onion, and chicken and sauté for 2 minutes, stirring occasionally. Turn the chicken over and let it cook for 2 more minutes.

3. Press Cancel and pour the broth into the pot. Using a wooden spoon, scrape up any browned bits stuck to the bottom of the pot. Add the soy sauce and honey and stir to combine.

4. Lock the lid into place. Select Pressure Cook or Manual; set the pressure to High and the time to 8 minutes. Make sure the steam release knob is in the sealed position. After cooking, naturally release the pressure for 10 minutes, then quick release any remaining pressure.

5. Unlock and remove the lid. Using a slotted spoon, transfer the chicken to a plate.

6. Select Sauté. Once the liquid starts bubbling, whisk in the cornstarch slurry and sesame oil. Whisk consistently for 2 minutes or until the sauce starts to thicken.

7. Serve immediately, or place the chicken in an airtight container and refrigerate for up to 4 days.

INGREDIENT VARIATION: *If you don't have sesame oil, you can use additional extra-virgin olive oil and top the chicken with toasted sesame seeds.*

GLUTEN-FREE OPTION: *Use tamari instead of soy sauce.*

INDIAN BUTTER CHICKEN

SERVES 6

PREP AND FINISHING:
10 MINUTES

SAUTÉ:
5 MINUTES

PRESSURE COOK:
10 MINUTES ON HIGH

RELEASE:
NATURAL FOR
10 MINUTES,
THEN QUICK

TOTAL TIME:
45 MINUTES

GLUTEN-FREE (SEE TIP)

PER SERVING
Calories: 319; Fat: 13g;
Carbohydrates: 14g;
Fiber: 4g; Protein: 39g;
Sodium: 357mg

When my husband and I were dating and living near Los Angeles, we used to go out for Indian food at least once a week. Butter chicken is one of our favorite dishes, so obviously I had to re-create it in the Instant Pot®. Don't worry, this dish is not too spicy. I love to serve it with basmati rice (page 20) to soak up the creamy flavors.

1 tablespoon extra-virgin olive oil
2 garlic cloves, minced
1 medium yellow onion, diced
1 tablespoon garam masala
¼ teaspoon ground ginger
1 cup low-sodium chicken broth
1 (6-ounce) can tomato paste
1 medium head cauliflower, cut into florets (about 3 cups)
2 pounds boneless, skinless chicken breasts (5 or 6 breasts)
2 tablespoons unsalted butter, cut into small pieces
½ cup full-fat canned coconut milk
½ teaspoon fine sea salt

1. Select Sauté and add the olive oil to the inner pot. Once the oil is hot, add the garlic, onion, garam masala, and ginger and sauté for 3 minutes, stirring occasionally.

2. Press Cancel and pour the broth into the pot. Using a wooden spoon, scrape up any browned bits stuck to the bottom of the pot. Add the tomato paste, cauliflower, and chicken to the pot, but do not stir. Top the chicken with the butter pieces.

3. Lock the lid into place. Select Pressure Cook or Manual; set the pressure to High and the time to 10 minutes. Make sure the steam release knob is in the sealed position. After cooking, naturally release the pressure for 10 minutes, then quick release any remaining pressure.

4. Unlock and remove the lid. Using a slotted spoon, transfer the chicken to a cutting board.

5. Use two forks to shred the chicken, then return it to the pot. Stir in the coconut milk and salt.

6. Serve immediately, or place the chicken in an airtight container and refrigerate for up to 4 days.

INGREDIENT VARIATION:
If you don't have garam masala, you can substitute with curry powder.

GLUTEN-FREE OPTION:
Make sure the tomato paste is gluten-free. Some brands are processed with gluten products.

TURKEY BOLOGNESE

SERVES 6

PREP AND FINISHING:
20 MINUTES

SAUTÉ:
10 MINUTES

PRESSURE COOK:
10 MINUTES ON HIGH

RELEASE:
NATURAL FOR
10 MINUTES,
THEN QUICK

TOTAL TIME:
60 MINUTES

DAIRY-FREE
FREEZER FRIENDLY
GLUTEN-FREE (SEE TIP)

PER SERVING
Calories: 279; Fat: 8g;
Carbohydrates: 12g;
Fiber: 4g; Protein: 38g;
Sodium: 257mg

If pasta night is a thing in your house like it is in mine, then you'll want to try this easy turkey Bolognese. The sauce has a super tomato flavor, and it's great over any type of pasta you like. For a spicy kick, add a pinch of red pepper flakes to the sauce just before serving.

2 tablespoons extra-virgin olive oil

1 medium yellow onion, chopped

2 garlic cloves, minced

2 carrots, peeled and diced (about 1 cup)

2 tablespoons tomato paste

½ cup red wine

2 pounds ground turkey

1 (28-ounce) can crushed tomatoes

½ cup water

1 teaspoon dried oregano

1. Select Sauté and add the olive oil to the inner pot. Once the oil is hot, add the onion, garlic, carrots, and tomato paste; sauté for 3 minutes or until the vegetables start to soften.

2. Pour the wine into the pot. Using a wooden spoon, scrape up any browned bits stuck to the bottom of the pot.

3. Add the ground turkey. Use the wooden spoon to break the meat apart as it cooks, about 3 minutes.

4. Press Cancel and add the crushed tomatoes, water, and oregano.

5. Lock the lid into place. Select Pressure Cook or Manual; set the pressure to High and the time to 10 minutes. Make sure the steam release knob is in the sealed position. After cooking, naturally release the pressure for 10 minutes, then quick release any remaining pressure.

6. Unlock and remove the lid. Stir the sauce. If you want to thicken the sauce, select Sauté and let the sauce simmer for about 10 minutes.

7. Serve immediately, or place the sauce in an airtight container and refrigerate for up to 4 days or freeze for up to 2 months.

INGREDIENT VARIATION: *You can use lean ground beef in this recipe instead of ground turkey.*

GLUTEN-FREE OPTION: *Make sure the tomato paste is gluten-free. Some brands are processed with gluten products.*

Sloppy Joes, page 152

7

Beef and Pork Mains

BEEF BURGUNDY

SERVES 8

PREP AND FINISHING:
10 MINUTES

SAUTÉ:
5 MINUTES

PRESSURE COOK:
30 MINUTES ON HIGH

RELEASE:
NATURAL FOR
10 MINUTES,
THEN QUICK

TOTAL TIME:
1 HOUR, 5 MINUTES

DAIRY-FREE
FREEZER FRIENDLY
GLUTEN-FREE (SEE TIP)

PER SERVING
Calories: 307; Fat: 11g;
Carbohydrates: 12g;
Fiber: 2g; Protein: 34g;
Sodium: 346mg

It's impossible not to love this dish once you see how easy it is to throw together. The red wine makes for a flavorful, elegant sauce that coats the beef and infuses every bite with robust flavor. This dish goes nicely with steamed broccoli or cauliflower and a baked potato on the side.

2 pounds beef chuck roast, cut into 1-inch cubes
¼ cup all-purpose flour
2 tablespoons extra-virgin olive oil
2 garlic cloves, minced
1 medium yellow onion, diced
1 teaspoon dried thyme
1 teaspoon fine sea salt
½ teaspoon freshly ground black pepper
1 cup red wine
1 tablespoon tomato paste
4 carrots, peeled and sliced (about 1 cup)

1. Place the beef and flour in a zip-top bag. Seal the bag and then use your hands to make sure the beef gets coated with the flour.

2. Select Sauté and add the olive oil to the inner pot. Once the oil is hot, add the flour-coated beef, garlic, onion, thyme, salt, and pepper; sauté for 3 minutes, stirring occasionally.

3. Press Cancel and pour in the wine. Using a wooden spoon, scrape up any browned bits stuck to the bottom of the pot. Add the tomato paste and carrots and stir to combine.

4. Lock the lid into place. Select Pressure Cook or Manual; set the pressure to High and the time to 30 minutes. Make sure the steam release knob is in the sealed position. After cooking, naturally release the pressure for 10 minutes, then quick release any remaining pressure.

5. Unlock and remove the lid. Serve immediately, or place the beef and sauce in an airtight container and refrigerate for up to 4 days or freeze for up to 2 months.

COOKING TIP: *You can use celery or zucchini instead of carrots. If you don't have red wine, you can use low-sodium beef broth instead.*

GLUTEN-FREE OPTION: *Use your favorite gluten-free flour blend instead of all-purpose flour. Also make sure the tomato paste is gluten-free. Some brands are processed with gluten products.*

BEEF STROGANOFF WITH SPRING GREEN PEAS

SERVES 6

PREP AND FINISHING:
15 MINUTES

SAUTÉ:
10 MINUTES

PRESSURE COOK:
10 MINUTES ON HIGH

RELEASE:
NATURAL FOR
10 MINUTES,
THEN QUICK

TOTAL TIME:
55 MINUTES

**ADVANCE PREP
(SEE TIP)**

GLUTEN-FREE (SEE TIP)

PER SERVING
Calories: 306; Fat: 11g;
Carbohydrates: 12g;
Fiber: 3g; Protein: 39g;
Sodium: 157mg

Beef Stroganoff is traditionally a heavy meal, but it's just so darned tasty! Here I've created a lightened up version using yogurt instead of sour cream and a generous serving of green peas. The sauce is creamy with a distinctive tangy flavor. Serve this dish over traditional egg noodles, or try it over brown rice (page 22) or steamed potatoes.

2 tablespoons cornstarch

½ cup water

2 tablespoons extra-virgin olive oil

2 pounds sirloin steak, cut into thin strips

3 garlic cloves, minced

2 shallots, diced

2 cups button mushrooms, sliced

1 cup low-sodium beef broth

2 cups green peas (thawed if frozen)

2 tablespoons Dijon mustard

¼ cup chopped fresh dill

⅓ cup low-fat plain Greek yogurt

Juice of 1 medium lemon

1. In a small bowl, make a slurry by whisking together the cornstarch and water. Set aside.

2. Select Sauté and add the olive oil to the inner pot. Once the oil is hot, use tongs to place the beef strips into the pot. Cook the beef, stirring constantly, for 2 minutes or until it starts to brown. Add the garlic, shallots, and mushrooms and stir to combine.

3. Press Cancel and add the broth. Using a wooden spoon, scrape up any browned bits stuck to the bottom of the pot.

4. Lock the lid into place. Select Pressure Cook or Manual; set the pressure to High and the time to 10 minutes. Make sure the steam release knob is in the sealed position. After cooking, naturally release the pressure for 10 minutes, then quick release any remaining pressure.

5. Unlock and remove the lid. Select Sauté.

6. Add the peas, cornstarch slurry, and mustard and whisk to combine. Continue whisking for about 2 minutes or until the sauce starts to thicken. Press Cancel and stir in the dill, yogurt, and lemon juice.

7. Serve immediately, or place the stroganoff in an airtight container and refrigerate for up to 4 days.

ADVANCE PREP TIP: *Slice the beef and refrigerate it in an airtight container for up to 2 days. You can also prepare the garlic, shallots, and mushrooms up to a week in advance; store them all together in an airtight container and refrigerate until you're ready to cook.*

GLUTEN-FREE OPTION: *Be sure to use Dijon mustard that is labeled gluten-free.*

BARBACOA BEEF

SERVES 8

PREP AND FINISHING:
10 MINUTES

SAUTÉ:
5 MINUTES

PRESSURE COOK:
30 MINUTES ON HIGH

RELEASE:
NATURAL FOR
10 MINUTES,
THEN QUICK

TOTAL TIME:
1 HOUR, 5 MINUTES

DAIRY-FREE
FREEZER FRIENDLY
GLUTEN-FREE

PER SERVING
Calories: 256; Fat: 4g;
Carbohydrates: 3g;
Fiber: 0g; Protein: 31g;
Sodium: 391mg

Barbacoa beef is a potluck favorite that feeds a crowd. It also works great for meal prepping because it's so versatile. Serve it in tacos, burritos, or enchiladas, or spoon it on top of a big green salad. The spicy beef soaks up all the flavor from the green chiles and comes out fork-tender and melt-in-your-mouth delicious.

2 tablespoons extra-virgin olive oil
2 pounds beef chuck roast, cut into 2-inch cubes
2 garlic cloves, minced
1 medium yellow onion, diced
1 teaspoon ground cumin
½ teaspoon dried oregano
½ teaspoon chili powder
1 teaspoon fine sea salt
½ teaspoon freshly ground black pepper
1 cup low-sodium beef broth
Juice of 2 limes
1 (4-ounce) can diced green chiles

1. Select Sauté and add the olive oil to the inner pot. Once the oil is hot, add the beef, garlic, onion, cumin, oregano, chili powder, salt, and pepper; sauté for 3 minutes, stirring occasionally.

2. Press Cancel and pour in the broth, lime juice, and green chiles. Using a wooden spoon, scrape up any browned bits stuck to the bottom of the pot.

3. Lock the lid into place. Select Pressure Cook or Manual; set the pressure to High and the time to 30 minutes. Make sure the steam release knob is in the sealed position. After cooking, naturally release the pressure for 10 minutes, then quick release any remaining pressure.

4. Unlock and remove the lid. Stir the mixture. If you want to shred the beef, use two forks to pull apart each piece.

5. Serve immediately, or place the beef in an airtight container and refrigerate for up to 4 days or freeze for up to 2 months.

COOKING TIP: *You can use whatever cut of beef you prefer, but chuck roast is an affordable cut with lots of flavor. Trim off any visible fat before cooking.*

INGREDIENT VARIATION: *If you like spicy food, you can add up to ¼ teaspoon of cayenne pepper with the other spices.*

POT ROAST WITH CARROTS AND POTATOES

SERVES 6

PREP AND FINISHING:
10 MINUTES

SAUTÉ:
5 MINUTES

PRESSURE COOK:
40 MINUTES ON HIGH

RELEASE:
NATURAL FOR
10 MINUTES,
THEN QUICK

TOTAL TIME:
1 HOUR, 15 MINUTES

DAIRY-FREE
FREEZER FRIENDLY
GLUTEN-FREE (SEE TIP)

PER SERVING
Calories: 362; Fat: 14g;
Carbohydrates: 24g;
Fiber: 3g; Protein: 34g;
Sodium: 521mg

This is one of my all-time favorite Instant Pot® recipes. I mostly make it on Sundays for a nice dinner, but it almost feels like cheating because it's so simple to throw together. I like to serve this dish with a fresh green salad on the side.

2 tablespoons extra-virgin olive oil

1 (2-pound) beef chuck roast

2 garlic cloves, minced

1 medium yellow onion, diced

2 cups low-sodium beef broth

4 large carrots, peeled and cut into 2-inch pieces

1½ pounds medium red potatoes, quartered

½ teaspoon dried oregano

2 teaspoons Worcestershire sauce

2 bay leaves

1 teaspoon fine sea salt

½ teaspoon freshly ground black pepper

1. Select Sauté and add the olive oil to the inner pot. Once the oil is hot, add the beef, garlic, and onion and cook for 3 minutes, turning the beef once so it browns on both sides.

2. Press Cancel and pour in the broth. Using a wooden spoon, scrape up any browned bits stuck to the bottom of the pot. Add the carrots, potatoes, oregano, Worcestershire sauce, bay leaves, salt, and pepper; stir to combine.

3. Lock the lid into place. Select Pressure Cook or Manual; set the pressure to High and the time to 40 minutes. Make sure the steam release knob is in the sealed position. After cooking, naturally release the pressure for 10 minutes, then quick release any remaining pressure.

4. Unlock and remove the lid. Stir the ingredients. Use tongs to remove and discard the bay leaves. If you want to shred the beef, use tongs to transfer it to a cutting board and two forks to shred the meat. Return the meat to the pot.

5. Serve immediately, or place the pot roast in an airtight container and refrigerate for up to 4 days or freeze for up to 2 months.

COOKING TIP: *You can use whatever beef roast you like, but chuck roast is an affordable cut with lots of flavor. Trim off any visible fat before cooking.*

GLUTEN-FREE OPTION: *Make sure you use Worcestershire sauce that is labeled gluten-free.*

SLOPPY JOES

SERVES 8

PREP AND FINISHING:
5 MINUTES

SAUTÉ:
5 MINUTES

PRESSURE COOK:
10 MINUTES ON HIGH

RELEASE:
NATURAL FOR
10 MINUTES,
THEN QUICK

TOTAL TIME:
40 MINUTES

DAIRY-FREE
FREEZER FRIENDLY
GLUTEN-FREE (SEE TIP)
ONE POT

PER SERVING
Calories: 246; Fat: 12g;
Carbohydrates: 7g;
Fiber: 1g; Protein: 24g;
Sodium: 400mg

These Sloppy Joes are perfect for those evenings when you don't have anything planned but need dinner on the table fast. You just need to add the meat and spices and let the Instant Pot® do all the work. These Sloppy Joes can be served on hamburger buns or on top of sweet potatoes (page 27) or mashed potatoes.

1 tablespoon extra-virgin olive oil
2 pounds 90% lean ground beef
1 teaspoon onion powder
½ teaspoon garlic powder
1 teaspoon chili powder
1 (16-ounce) can tomato purée
½ cup ketchup
2 tablespoons reduced-sodium soy sauce
1 tablespoon brown sugar
Purple slaw, for garnish (optional)
Fresh chopped parsley, for garnish (optional)

1. Select Sauté and add the olive oil to the inner pot. Once the oil is hot, add the ground beef and cook for 3 minutes, using a spatula to break up the meat.

2. Press Cancel and add the onion powder, garlic powder, chili powder, tomato purée, ketchup, soy sauce, and brown sugar. Stir to combine.

3. Lock the lid into place. Select Pressure Cook or Manual; set the pressure to High and the time to 10 minutes. Make sure the steam release knob is in the sealed position. After cooking, naturally release the pressure for 10 minutes, then quick release the remaining pressure.

4. Unlock and remove the lid. Stir the Sloppy Joe mixture to make sure it's well combined.

5. Serve immediately garnished with purple slaw and parsley, if desired, or place the Sloppy Joes in an airtight container and refrigerate for up to 4 days or freeze for up to 2 months.

MEAL PREP TIP: *The meat has a ton of flavor, so it's great for leftovers. Besides serving it on a bun or over potatoes, you can also serve it on top of a salad for a low-carb option.*

GLUTEN-FREE OPTION: *Use tamari in place of the soy sauce.*

BROCCOLI BEEF

SERVES 6

PREP AND FINISHING:
20 MINUTES

SAUTÉ:
10 MINUTES

PRESSURE COOK:
8 MINUTES PLUS
1 MINUTE ON HIGH

RELEASE:
NATURAL FOR
5 MINUTES,
THEN QUICK

TOTAL TIME:
54 MINUTES

DAIRY-FREE
GLUTEN-FREE (SEE TIP)
ONE POT

PER SERVING
Calories: 330; Fat: 16g;
Carbohydrates: 10g;
Fiber: 2g; Protein: 35g;
Sodium: 540mg

The sauce for this beef and broccoli dish is spicy and sweet, and it coats the sizzling beef and tender broccoli florets, making it the star of every bite. You can serve this dish right out of the pot or spoon it over brown rice (page 22) or basmati rice (page 20).

2 tablespoons cornstarch

½ cup water

1 tablespoon extra-virgin olive oil

2 pounds flank steak, cut into ½-inch-thick slices

3 garlic cloves, minced

½ cup low-sodium beef broth

⅓ cup reduced-sodium soy sauce

¼ cup white wine vinegar

1 tablespoon brown sugar

2 teaspoons Sriracha sauce

¼ teaspoon ground ginger

1 pound broccoli florets, fresh or frozen (about 3½ cups)

4 scallions, white and light green parts only, sliced, for garnish

1. In a small bowl, make a slurry by whisking together the cornstarch and water. Set aside.

2. Select Sauté and add the olive oil to the inner pot. Once the oil is hot, add the steak and garlic and sauté for 3 minutes, stirring occasionally so the beef starts to brown on both sides.

3. Press Cancel and add the broth. Using a wooden spoon, scrape up any browned bits stuck to the bottom of the pot. Add the soy sauce, vinegar, brown sugar, Sriracha, and ginger; stir to combine.

4. Lock the lid into place. Select Pressure Cook or Manual; set the pressure to High and the time to 8 minutes. Make sure the steam release knob is in the sealed position. After cooking, naturally release the pressure for 5 minutes, then quick release any remaining pressure.

5. Unlock and remove the lid. Add the broccoli florets.

6. Lock the lid into place again. Select Pressure Cook or Manual; set the pressure to High and the time to 1 minute. Make sure the steam release knob is in the sealed position. After cooking, quick release the pressure.

7. Unlock and remove the lid. Select Sauté. Use a slotted spoon to transfer the beef and broccoli to a serving plate.

8. Once the liquid is bubbling in the inner pot, whisk in the cornstarch slurry and let the sauce cook, uncovered, for 2 minutes or until it starts to thicken.

9. Return the beef and broccoli to the pot and stir to combine.

10. Serve the dish garnished with the scallions. Place leftovers in an airtight container and refrigerate for up to 4 days.

INGREDIENT VARIATION: *You can use cauliflower florets instead of broccoli florets if you prefer.*

GLUTEN-FREE OPTION: *Use tamari in place of the soy sauce.*

KOREAN BEEF BOWL

SERVES 6

PREP AND FINISHING:
15 MINUTES

SAUTÉ:
10 MINUTES

PRESSURE COOK:
10 MINUTES ON HIGH

RELEASE:
NATURAL FOR
5 MINUTES,
THEN QUICK

TOTAL TIME:
50 MINUTES

DAIRY-FREE
GLUTEN-FREE (SEE TIP)
ONE POT

PER SERVING
Calories: 355; Fat: 16g;
Carbohydrates: 16g;
Fiber: 1g; Protein: 36g;
Sodium: 714mg

I crave these Korean Beef Bowls on a weekly basis. The sliced meat is spicy and tender and goes perfectly with crisp cucumber and red bell pepper slices. It's traditional to serve the meat on a bed of steamed white rice, but you can also serve it with sautéed cauliflower rice for a lower-carb option. Either way, you won't be disappointed with this flavorful dish.

2 tablespoons cornstarch

½ cup water

1 tablespoon extra-virgin olive oil

2 pounds flank steak, sliced into ½-inch-thick strips

3 garlic cloves, minced

½ cup low-sodium beef broth

⅓ cup reduced-sodium soy sauce

¼ cup white wine vinegar

2 tablespoons honey

2 teaspoons Sriracha sauce

¼ teaspoon ground ginger

1 medium cucumber, sliced

2 red bell peppers, seeded and sliced

4 scallions, white and light green parts only, sliced

KOREAN BEEF BOWL *continues*

1. In a small bowl make a slurry by whisking together the cornstarch and water. Set aside.

2. Select Sauté and add the olive oil to the inner pot. Once the oil is hot, add the steak and garlic and sauté for 3 minutes, stirring occasionally so the beef starts to brown on all sides.

3. Press Cancel and add the broth. Using a wooden spoon, scrape up any browned bits stuck to the bottom of the pot. Add the soy sauce, vinegar, honey, Sriracha, and ginger; stir to combine.

4. Lock the lid into place. Select Pressure Cook or Manual; set the pressure to High and the time to 10 minutes. Make sure the steam release knob is in the sealed position. After cooking, naturally release the pressure for 5 minutes, then quick release any remaining pressure.

5. Unlock and remove the lid. Select Sauté. Use a slotted spoon to transfer the beef to a serving plate.

6. Once the liquid begins to bubble, whisk in the cornstarch slurry and let the sauce cook, uncovered, for 2 minutes or until it starts to thicken. Return the beef to the pot and stir to combine.

7. Serve each bowl with a few slices of cucumber and red bell pepper and some sliced scallions on top. Place leftovers in an airtight container and refrigerate for up to 4 days.

MEAL PREP TIP: *Store the cucumber slices, red bell pepper slices, and sliced scallions in separate air-tight containers. Reheat the beef, then top with the fresh vegetables just before serving.*

GLUTEN-FREE OPTION: *Use tamari in place of the soy sauce.*

MONGOLIAN BEEF AND BROCCOLI

SERVES 6

PREP AND FINISHING:
10 MINUTES

SAUTÉ:
5 MINUTES

PRESSURE COOK:
10 MINUTES PLUS
1 MINUTE ON HIGH

RELEASE:
NATURAL FOR
5 MINUTES,
THEN QUICK

TOTAL TIME:
41 MINUTES

DAIRY-FREE
FREEZER FRIENDLY
GLUTEN-FREE (SEE TIP)
ONE POT

PER SERVING
Calories: 321; Fat: 14g;
Carbohydrates: 10g;
Fiber: 2g; Protein: 37g;
Sodium: 600mg

I always enjoy Mongolian beef and broccoli when we eat out, but it certainly doesn't count as a healthy food choice. So you can imagine my excitement when I finally created a more nutritious version that fits into my clean-eating lifestyle. The beef is tender and full of sweet and tangy flavor, and the broccoli is crisp and bright green. I like to serve this recipe with cooked basmati rice (page 20).

2 tablespoons cornstarch

½ cup water

2 tablespoons extra-virgin olive oil

2 pounds skirt steak, cut into thin strips

1 medium yellow onion, chopped

2 garlic cloves, minced

1 cup low-sodium beef broth

¼ cup reduced-sodium soy sauce

2 tablespoons balsamic vinegar

2 tablespoons brown sugar

15 ounces broccoli florets, fresh or frozen

1. In a small bowl, make a slurry by whisking together the cornstarch and water. Set aside.

2. Select Sauté and add the olive oil. Once the oil is hot, add the steak, onion, and garlic; cook for about 3 minutes, stirring occasionally.

3. Press Cancel and add the broth, soy sauce, vinegar, and brown sugar; stir to combine. Using a wooden spoon, scrape up any browned bits stuck to the bottom of the pot.

4. Lock the lid into place. Select Pressure Cook or Manual; set the pressure to High and the time to 10 minutes. Make sure the steam release knob is in the sealed position. After cooking, naturally release the pressure for 5 minutes, then quick release any remaining pressure.

5. Unlock and remove the lid. Add the broccoli florets.

6. Lock the lid into place again. Select Pressure Cook or Manual; set the pressure to High and the time to 1 minute (3 minutes if using frozen florets). Make sure the steam release knob is in the sealed position. After cooking, quick release the pressure.

7. Unlock and remove the lid. Select Sauté. Use a slotted spoon to transfer the beef and vegetables to a serving bowl.

8. Whisk the cornstarch slurry into the liquid. Let it cook, uncovered, for 2 minutes or until the sauce starts to thicken. Press Cancel. Add the beef and vegetables back to the pot and stir to combine.

9. Serve immediately, or place the beef and vegetables in an airtight container and refrigerate for up to 4 days or freeze for up to 2 months.

MEAL PREP TIP: *You can substitute cauliflower florets for the broccoli if you prefer.*

GLUTEN-FREE OPTION: *Use tamari in place of the soy sauce.*

ALL-IN-ONE MEATLOAF WITH MASHED POTATOES

SERVES 8

PREP AND FINISHING:
10 MINUTES

PRESSURE COOK:
30 MINUTES ON HIGH

RELEASE:
NATURAL FOR
10 MINUTES,
THEN QUICK

TOTAL TIME:
60 MINUTES

**ADVANCE PREP
(SEE TIP)
FREEZER FRIENDLY
GLUTEN-FREE (SEE TIP)
ONE POT**

PER SERVING
Calories: 286; Fat: 14g;
Carbohydrates: 12g;
Fiber: 1g; Protein: 25g;
Sodium: 370mg

Meatloaf with mashed potatoes is one of my ultimate comfort foods. And with the Instant Pot®, I can make both at the same time! The meatloaf is perfectly cooked with lots of tangy flavor, and the mashed potatoes are soft and fluffy. For me, nothing's better than a one-and-done meal like this recipe.

1 pound medium russet or Yukon Gold potatoes
1 cup low-sodium chicken broth
2 pounds 90% lean ground beef
½ medium yellow onion, chopped
2 garlic cloves, minced
1 egg
2 teaspoons Worcestershire sauce
1 teaspoon Dijon mustard
2 tablespoons unsalted butter
1 teaspoon fine sea salt
½ teaspoon freshly ground black pepper

1. Place the potatoes and broth in the inner pot.

2. In a large bowl, combine the ground beef, onion, garlic, egg, Worcestershire sauce, and mustard. Using your hands, mix the ingredients together thoroughly.

3. Form the meatloaf mixture into a loaf that will fit inside the inner pot.

4. Tear off a 2-foot piece of aluminum foil and fold it in half. Turn up the edges so it makes the shape of a square basket that will fit inside the inner pot. Place the meatloaf in the foil basket and place it on top of the potatoes.

5. Lock the lid into place. Select Pressure Cook or Manual; set the pressure to High and the time to 30 minutes. Make sure the steam release knob is in the sealed position. After cooking, naturally release the pressure for 10 minutes, then quick release the remaining pressure.

6. Unlock and remove the lid. Carefully remove the meatloaf and the foil from the pot. Add the butter, salt, and pepper to the potatoes, then mash them to your liking with a potato masher or immersion blender.

7. Serve immediately, or place the meatloaf and mashed potatoes in separate airtight containers and refrigerate for up to 4 days or freeze for up to 2 months.

ADVANCE PREP TIP: *You can prepare the meatloaf mixture up to 2 days in advance. Store it in an airtight container in the refrigerator until you're ready to cook.*

GLUTEN-FREE OPTION: *Be sure to use Dijon mustard and Worcestershire sauce that is labeled gluten-free.*

HAWAIIAN PINEAPPLE PORK

SERVES 6

PREP AND FINISHING:
10 MINUTES

SAUTÉ:
5 MINUTES

PRESSURE COOK:
10 MINUTES ON HIGH

RELEASE:
NATURAL FOR
10 MINUTES,
THEN QUICK

TOTAL TIME:
45 MINUTES

**ADVANCE PREP
(SEE TIP)**
DAIRY-FREE
GLUTEN-FREE (SEE TIP)

PER SERVING
Calories: 343; Fat: 16g;
Carbohydrates: 23g;
Fiber: 2g; Protein: 30g;
Sodium: 824mg

Pineapple and pork make a classic pairing and go together so nicely in this easy recipe. The pork is tender and perfectly cooked, and the sweet and tangy pineapple adds a ton of flavor. The pineapple juice and brown sugar create a sticky sweet sauce that coats the pork and veggies. I like to serve this dish over brown rice (page 22) or basmati rice (page 20).

2 tablespoons extra-virgin olive oil

2 pounds pork loin, cut into 1-inch chunks

1 medium yellow onion, chopped

3 garlic cloves, minced

1 (20-ounce) can pineapple chunks in juice

2 red bell peppers, seeded and chopped

¼ cup reduced-sodium soy sauce

2 tablespoons brown sugar

¼ teaspoon chili powder

1. Select Sauté and add the olive oil to the inner pot. Once the oil is hot, add the pork, onion, and garlic; sauté for 4 minutes, stirring occasionally to brown the pork on all sides.

2. Press Cancel and add the pineapple and its juice. Using a wooden spoon, scrape up any browned bits stuck to the bottom of the pot. Add the bell peppers, soy sauce, brown sugar, and chili powder. Stir to combine.

3. Lock the lid into place. Select Pressure Cook or Manual; set the pressure to High and the time to 10 minutes. Make sure the steam release knob is in the sealed position. After cooking, naturally release the pressure for 10 minutes, then quick release any remaining pressure.

4. Unlock and remove the lid. Serve immediately, or place the pork and vegetables in an airtight container and refrigerate for up to 4 days.

ADVANCE PREP TIP: *Prep the pork and vegetables up to 2 days in advance. Store them in separate airtight containers until you're ready to cook. If you plan to serve this with rice, cook the rice up to 5 days in advance, refrigerate it in an airtight container, and reheat it just before serving.*

GLUTEN-FREE OPTION: *Use tamari in place of the soy sauce.*

HONEY MUSTARD PORK TENDERLOIN

SERVES 6

PREP AND FINISHING:
10 MINUTES

SAUTÉ:
10 MINUTES

PRESSURE COOK:
8 MINUTES ON HIGH

RELEASE:
NATURAL FOR
10 MINUTES,
THEN QUICK

TOTAL TIME:
48 MINUTES

DAIRY-FREE
GLUTEN-FREE (SEE TIP)

PER SERVING
Calories: 283; Fat: 10g;
Carbohydrates: 15g;
Fiber: 1g; Protein: 32g;
Sodium: 306mg

You'll look like a gourmet chef with this pork tenderloin recipe. I made it for a dinner party, and everyone thought I had spent hours in the kitchen. I think the sauce is the magic component: it's sweet and tangy, with just enough heat from the Dijon mustard.

2 tablespoons cornstarch

½ cup water

2 tablespoons extra-virgin olive oil

2 pounds pork tenderloin

1 cup low-sodium chicken broth

3 garlic cloves, minced

2 tablespoons Dijon mustard

¼ cup honey

½ teaspoon fine sea salt

¼ teaspoon freshly ground black pepper

1. In a small bowl, make a slurry by whisking together the cornstarch and water. Set aside.

2. Select Sauté and add the olive oil to the inner pot. Once the oil is hot, add the pork and brown it for 2 minutes per side.

3. Press Cancel. Using tongs, transfer the pork to a plate.

4. Pour the broth into the pot. Using a wooden spoon, scrape up any browned bits stuck to the bottom of the pot. Add the garlic, mustard, honey, salt, and pepper; stir to combine. Place the trivet inside the pot. Use the tongs to place the pork on the trivet.

5. Lock the lid into place. Select Pressure Cook or Manual; set the pressure to High and the time to 8 minutes. Make sure the steam release knob is in the sealed position. After cooking, naturally release the pressure for 10 minutes, then quick release any remaining pressure.

6. Unlock and remove the lid. Select Sauté. Using clean tongs, transfer the pork to a cutting board.

7. Whisk the cornstarch slurry into the liquid and cook, uncovered, for about 5 minutes or until the sauce starts to thicken. Carefully pour the sauce into a small pitcher or glass bowl.

8. Using a sharp knife, slice the pork into 6 servings. Serve the pork with the sauce. Place leftovers in an airtight container and refrigerate for up to 4 days.

MEAL PREP TIP: *Serve this dish with whatever side dish you like, such as cooked brown rice (page 22), quinoa (page 23), steamed vegetables (page 18), or mashed potatoes.*

GLUTEN-FREE OPTION: *Be sure to use Dijon mustard that is labeled gluten-free.*

PORK CARNITAS

SERVES 6

PREP AND FINISHING:
10 MINUTES

SAUTÉ:
10 MINUTES

PRESSURE COOK:
60 MINUTES ON HIGH

RELEASE:
NATURAL FOR
10 MINUTES,
THEN QUICK

TOTAL TIME:
1 HOUR, 40 MINUTES

DAIRY-FREE
FREEZER FRIENDLY
GLUTEN-FREE

PER SERVING
Calories: 247; Fat: 11g;
Carbohydrates: 1g;
Fiber: 0g; Protein: 35g;
Sodium: 403mg

I appreciate the slow cooking of pork for traditional carnitas, but with the Instant Pot® I get tender pork and amazing flavors in a fraction of the time. The meat shreds easily and is perfect for making tacos, burritos, and salads. There's just enough spice to delight but not overpower your taste buds.

2 tablespoons extra-virgin olive oil

2 pounds boneless pork roast, cut into 2 or 3 pieces so it fits inside the pot

1 cup low-sodium chicken broth

1 teaspoon fine sea salt

½ teaspoon freshly ground black pepper

1 teaspoon ground cumin

1 teaspoon dried oregano

1 teaspoon chili powder

½ teaspoon garlic powder

Juice of 2 limes

1. Select Sauté and add the olive oil to the inner pot. Once the oil is hot, add the pork and brown it for 3 minutes. Turn the pieces over and brown for another 3 minutes.

2. Press Cancel and pour in the broth. Using a wooden spoon, scrape up any browned bits stuck to the bottom of the pot. Add the salt, pepper, cumin, oregano, chili powder, and garlic powder; stir to combine.

3. Lock the lid into place. Select Pressure Cook or Manual; set the pressure to High and the time to 60 minutes. Make sure the steam release knob is in the sealed position. After cooking, naturally release the pressure for 10 minutes, then quick release any remaining pressure.

4. Unlock and remove the lid. Stir in the lime juice. Using two forks, shred the pork. Serve immediately, or place the shredded pork in an airtight container and refrigerate for up to 4 days or freeze for up to 2 months.

COOKING TIP: *Pork shoulder, butt roast, or shoulder blade roast work best for this recipe.*

SWEET AND SOUR PORK

SERVES 6

PREP AND FINISHING:
15 MINUTES

SAUTÉ:
10 MINUTES

PRESSURE COOK:
8 MINUTES ON HIGH

RELEASE:
NATURAL FOR
10 MINUTES,
THEN QUICK

TOTAL TIME:
53 MINUTES

DAIRY-FREE
FREEZER FRIENDLY
GLUTEN-FREE (SEE TIP)

PER SERVING
Calories: 332; Fat: 9g;
Carbohydrates: 27g;
Fiber: 1g; Protein: 36g;
Sodium: 553mg

There are some days when it's really hard to resist grabbing takeout from the nearest restaurant. This recipe is a healthier version of one of my favorite takeout meals, featuring tender pork coated with a delicious orange sauce. I'm always happier when I resist the urge to order out and cook at home instead, and the leftovers from this recipe are even more delicious the next day.

2 tablespoons cornstarch

½ cup water

1 tablespoon extra-virgin olive oil

2 pounds boneless pork shoulder, cut into 1-inch pieces

1 medium yellow onion, chopped

2 garlic cloves, minced

1¼ cups freshly squeezed orange juice

2 tablespoons tomato paste

⅓ cup reduced-sodium soy sauce

¼ cup white wine vinegar

¼ cup honey

2 red bell peppers, seeded and sliced

1. In a small bowl, make a slurry by whisking together the cornstarch and water. Set aside.

2. Select Sauté and add the olive oil. Once the oil is hot, add the pork, onion, and garlic and sauté for 3 minutes, stirring occasionally.

3. Press Cancel and add the orange juice. Using a wooden spoon, scrape up any browned bits stuck to the bottom of the pot. Add the tomato paste, soy sauce, vinegar, honey, and bell peppers; stir to combine.

4. Lock the lid into place. Select Pressure Cook or Manual; set the pressure to High and the time to 8 minutes. Make sure the steam release knob is in the sealed position. After cooking, naturally release the pressure for 10 minutes, then quick release any remaining pressure.

5. Unlock and remove the lid. Select Sauté. Using a slotted spoon, transfer the pork and vegetables to a serving bowl.

6. Whisk the cornstarch slurry into the liquid and let it simmer, uncovered, for 2 minutes or until the sauce starts to thicken.

7. Place the pork and vegetables back in the pot and stir to combine. Serve immediately, or place the pork and vegetables in an airtight container and refrigerate for up to 4 days or freeze up to 2 months.

MEAL PREP TIP: *Serve this dish with whatever side dish you like, such as cooked brown rice (page 22), quinoa (page 23), steamed vegetables (page 18), or mashed potatoes.*

GLUTEN-FREE OPTION: *Use tamari in place of the soy sauce.*

TANGY VINEGAR PORK WITH POTATOES

SERVES 6

PREP AND FINISHING:
15 MINUTES

SAUTÉ:
10 MINUTES

PRESSURE COOK:
25 MINUTES ON HIGH

RELEASE:
NATURAL FOR
10 MINUTES,
THEN QUICK

TOTAL TIME:
1 HOUR, 10 MINUTES

DAIRY-FREE
GLUTEN-FREE (SEE TIP)
ONE POT

PER SERVING
Calories: 318; Fat: 8g;
Carbohydrates: 22g;
Fiber: 2g; Protein: 37g;
Sodium: 554mg

This dish is inspired by a Filipino dish that is made by cooking meat with vinegar, soy sauce, garlic, and peppercorns. It's super tangy, slightly sweet, and delicious. I added potatoes here to make it a full meal. It's traditional to serve this dish on top of shredded cabbage or thinly sliced baby bok choy.

2 tablespoons cornstarch

½ cup water

1 tablespoon extra-virgin olive oil

2 pounds boneless pork shoulder, cut into 1-inch cubes

2 garlic cloves, minced

1¼ cups low-sodium chicken broth

⅓ cup reduced-sodium soy sauce

¼ cup white wine vinegar

2 tablespoons honey

½ teaspoon freshly ground black pepper

1 pound white potatoes, cut into 1-inch cubes

1. In a small bowl, make a slurry by whisking together the cornstarch and water. Set aside.

2. Select Sauté and add the olive oil. Once the oil is hot, add the pork and garlic and sauté for 3 minutes, stirring occasionally.

3. Press Cancel and pour in the broth. Using a wooden spoon, scrape up any browned bits stuck to the bottom of the pot. Add the soy sauce, vinegar, honey, black pepper, and potatoes to the pot; stir to combine.

4. Lock the lid into place. Select Pressure Cook or Manual; set the pressure to High and the time to 25 minutes. Make sure the steam release knob is in the sealed position. After cooking, naturally release the pressure for 10 minutes, then quick release any remaining pressure.

5. Unlock and remove the lid. Select Sauté. Using a slotted spoon, transfer the pork and potatoes to a serving plate.

6. Once the liquid in the pot is bubbling, whisk in the cornstarch slurry. Let the sauce simmer, uncovered, for about 2 minutes or until the sauce starts to thicken.

7. Return the pork and potatoes to the pot and stir to combine. Serve immediately, or place the pork and potatoes in an airtight container and refrigerate for up to 4 days.

MEAL PREP TIP: *Serve any leftovers with a wedge of fresh lime to squeeze on top before eating. This helps bring out the flavors of the sauce.*

GLUTEN-FREE OPTION: *Use tamari in place of the soy sauce.*

POLISH SAUSAGE WITH SAUERKRAUT

SERVES 6

PREP AND FINISHING:
10 MINUTES

SAUTÉ:
5 MINUTES

PRESSURE COOK:
10 MINUTES ON HIGH

RELEASE:
NATURAL FOR
10 MINUTES,
THEN QUICK

TOTAL TIME:
45 MINUTES

DAIRY-FREE
GLUTEN-FREE (SEE TIP)
ONE POT

PER SERVING
Calories: 341; Fat: 19g;
Carbohydrates: 32g;
Fiber: 8g, Protein: 12g;
Sodium: 1526mg

My husband and I went on a river boat cruise through the German countryside a few summers ago. It was so fun touring the charming medieval villages and castles. In one village we ate sausages, watched a pretzel-making demonstration, and listened to polka music all at the same time. This dish is inspired by that trip.

1 tablespoon extra-virgin olive oil

1 medium yellow onion, chopped

2 garlic cloves, minced

2 cups low-sodium chicken broth

1 (12-ounce) package fully cooked Polish sausage, cut into 1-inch-thick slices

1 (32-ounce) jar sauerkraut

1 apple, chopped

3 medium red potatoes, chopped into bite-size pieces

1. Select Sauté and add the olive oil to the inner pot. Once the oil is hot, add the onion and garlic and sauté for 3 minutes, stirring occasionally.

2. Press Cancel and pour in the broth. Using a wooden spoon, scrape up any browned bits stuck to the bottom of the pot. Add the sausage slices, sauerkraut, apple, and potatoes; stir to combine.

3. Lock the lid into place. Select Pressure Cook or Manual; set the pressure to High and the time to 10 minutes. Make sure the steam release knob is in the sealed position. After cooking, naturally release the pressure for 10 minutes, then quick release any remaining pressure.

4. Unlock and remove the lid. Serve immediately, or place the sausages and veggies in an airtight container and refrigerate for up to 4 days.

GLUTEN-FREE OPTION: *Make sure the sausages are gluten-free. Some are made using gluten products.*

INSTANT POT® COOKING TIME CHARTS

BEANS AND LEGUMES

You can cook soaked or unsoaked beans in the Instant Pot® with great results. I recommend cooking a maximum of 2 cups of dried beans at a time.

To soak beans, place 2 cups of dried beans in a large bowl. Fill the bowl with water until the beans are covered by at least 2 inches. Let them soak for 8 to 12 hours. You do not need to soak lentils.

To cook soaked or unsoaked beans, rinse and drain them. Place the beans in a 6- or 8-quart Instant Pot® and add enough water to cover them by at least ½ inch. Cook on the High setting for the recommended time. After cooking, let the pressure release naturally for 10 minutes, then quick release any remaining pressure.

TYPE OF BEAN	COOKING TIME IN MINUTES FOR UNSOAKED	COOKING TIME IN MINUTES FOR SOAKED
Adzuki	25	15
Black	25	15
Black-eyed peas	25	15
Cannellini	40	25
Chickpeas (garbanzo beans)	40	25
Great northern	30	25
Kidney, red	30	25
Lentils, green or brown	20	N/A
Lentils, red or yellow	15	N/A
Navy	30	25
Pinto	30	25
Split peas	20	15

GRAINS

It's important to rinse grains in a fine-mesh strainer before adding them to the Instant Pot®. The amount of liquid called for in the following cooking chart assumes that you've rinsed the grains before cooking. This chart also assumes that you're cooking 2 cups of grains at a time, which will yield about 6 servings.

Cook grains on the High setting. After cooking, naturally release the pressure for 10 minutes, then quick release any remaining pressure. Drain any excess liquid before serving.

TYPE OF GRAIN OR PSEUDOGRAIN	LIQUID PER 2 CUPS OF GRAIN	MINUTES UNDER HIGH PRESSURE
Barley, pearl	5 cups	10
Buckwheat	3½ cups	2
Farro	4 cups	10
Millet	3 cups	9
Oats, rolled	3 cups	6
Oats, steel cut	3 cups	10
Quinoa	2 cups	1
Rice, brown (long-grain)	2 cups	22
Rice, white (long-grain)	2 cups	4
Wheat berries	6 cups	15
Wild rice	5 cups	25

MEAT & POULTRY

Meats should be cooked on the High setting with at least 1 cup of liquid. Pour the liquid into the inner pot, then place the trivet inside. Place the meat on the trivet. After cooking, naturally release the pressure for 10 minutes, then quick release any remaining pressure.

TYPE OF MEAT	MINUTES UNDER HIGH PRESSURE
Beef, ground	10
Beef, meatballs	15
Beef, stew meat	20
Beef, ribs	30
Beef, whole roast	40
Chicken, breasts	10
Chicken, whole	30
Pork, loin roast	60
Pork, ribs	25
Turkey, boneless breast	20
Turkey, bone-in breast	30
Turkey, leg	20

FISH AND SEAFOOD

Most fish and seafood should be cooked on the High setting using the quick release method to prevent overcooking. Pour the liquid into the inner pot, then place the trivet inside. Place the fish or seafood on the trivet.

This table assumes that you're cooking fresh fish and seafood. To cook from frozen, add 2 minutes to the cooking time on the High setting.

FISH/SEAFOOD	MINUTES UNDER PRESSURE	RELEASE
Crab	4	Quick
Fish fillet	3	Quick
Fish steak	4	Quick
Lobster	4	Quick
Mussels	3	Quick
Seafood soup	7	Quick
Shrimp	2	Quick

VEGETABLES

Most vegetables should be placed on the trivet or in a steaming basket inside the Instant Pot®. Always be sure to use at least 1 cup of liquid when cooking vegetables. Unless noted, naturally release the pressure for 10 minutes, then quick release the remaining pressure.

This table assumes you are using fresh vegetables. To cook from frozen, add 2 minutes to the cooking time on the High setting.

VEGETABLE	MINUTES UNDER HIGH PRESSURE	RELEASE
Artichoke, whole, large	15	Natural
Asparagus, whole or halved	2	Quick
Broccoli florets	1	Quick
Brussels sprouts, halved	3	Natural
Carrots, ½-inch slices	1	Quick
Cauliflower florets	1	Quick
Corn on the cob	4	Natural
Green beans, whole	3	Quick
Peas	2	Quick
Potatoes, red, gold, or white (small or medium, whole)	10	Natural
Spaghetti squash, halved lengthwise	7	Quick
Sweet potatoes, medium, whole	15	Natural

The Dirty Dozen™ and Clean Fifteen™

A nonprofit environmental watchdog organization called Environmental Working Group (EWG) looks at data supplied by the US Department of Agriculture (USDA) and the Food and Drug Administration (FDA) about pesticide residues. Each year it compiles a list of the best and worst pesticide loads found in commercial crops. You can use these lists to decide which fruits and vegetables to buy organic to minimize your exposure to pesticides and which produce is considered safe enough to buy conventionally. This does not mean they are pesticide-free, though, so wash these fruits and vegetables thoroughly. The list is updated annually, and you can find it online at EWG.org/FoodNews.

DIRTY DOZEN™

1. strawberries
2. spinach
3. nectarines
4. apples
5. grapes
6. peaches
7. cherries
8. pears
9. tomatoes
10. celery
11. potatoes
12. sweet bell peppers

†Additionally, nearly three-quarters of hot pepper samples contained pesticide residues.

CLEAN FIFTEEN™

1. avocados
2. sweet corn*
3. pineapples
4. cabbages
5. onions
6. sweet peas (frozen)
7. papayas*
8. asparagus
9. mangoes
10. eggplants
11. melons
12. kiwis
13. cantaloupes
14. cauliflower
15. broccoli

* A small amount of sweet corn, papaya, and summer squash sold in the United States is produced from genetically modified seeds. Buy organic varieties of these crops if you want to avoid genetically modified produce.

Measurement Conversions

VOLUME EQUIVALENTS (LIQUID)

US STANDARD	US STANDARD (OUNCES)	METRIC (APPROXIMATE)
2 tablespoons	1 fl. oz.	30 mL
¼ cup	2 fl. oz.	60 mL
½ cup	4 fl. oz.	120 mL
1 cup	8 fl. oz.	240 mL
1½ cups	12 fl. oz.	355 mL
2 cups or 1 pint	16 fl. oz.	475 mL
4 cups or 1 quart	32 fl. oz.	1 L
1 gallon	128 fl. oz.	4 L

OVEN TEMPERATURES

FAHRENHEIT (F)	CELSIUS (C) (APPROXIMATE)
250°F	120°C
300°F	150°C
325°F	165°C
350°F	180°C
375°F	190°C
400°F	200°C
425°F	220°C
450°F	230°C

VOLUME EQUIVALENTS (DRY)

US STANDARD	METRIC (APPROXIMATE)
⅛ teaspoon	0.5 mL
¼ teaspoon	1 mL
½ teaspoon	2 mL
¾ teaspoon	4 mL
1 teaspoon	5 mL
1 tablespoon	15 mL
¼ cup	59 mL
⅓ cup	79 mL
½ cup	118 mL
⅔ cup	156 mL
¾ cup	177 mL
1 cup	235 mL
2 cups or 1 pint	475 mL
3 cups	700 mL
4 cups or 1 quart	1 L

WEIGHT EQUIVALENTS

US STANDARD	METRIC (APPROXIMATE)
½ ounce	15 g
1 ounce	30 g
2 ounces	60 g
4 ounces	115 g
8 ounces	225 g
12 ounces	340 g
16 ounces or 1 pound	455 g

RECIPE INDEX

INDEX

ACKNOWLEDGMENTS

Thank you to my parents, sister, and family for always believing in me. I offer special thanks to both my virtual and real-life friends who support me on a daily basis. Last, I'd like to acknowledge my husband, Alan, for being the best friend, recipe tester, and cheerleader I ever could have imagined. I love you!

ABOUT THE AUTHOR

Carrie Forrest is a clean eating specialist and the creator of the website Clean Eating Kitchen, where she shares easy gluten-free and dairy-free recipes and resources. Carrie has a professional background in nonprofit hospital fundraising and earned a master's degree in business and entrepreneurship from the University of Southern California.

Carrie became interested in nutrition while struggling to heal from a variety of health issues, including thyroid disease, chronic migraines, PCOS, panic attacks, and multiple food sensitivities. She later earned a master's degree in public health nutrition from the University of Massachusetts, Amherst.

Carrie lives with her husband and two cats on California's beautiful central coast. When she's not testing, filming, and photographing recipes for her blog, she enjoys visiting farmers' markets, hiking, and learning to play the violin. Follow Carrie on her blog, CleanEatingKitchen.com, on YouTube at Clean Eating Kitchen, or on Instagram @cleaneatingcarrie.